ALL THUMBS

Guide to
Compact Disc Players

Other All Thumbs Guides

Guide to
Compact Disc
Players

Gene B. Williams
Illustrations by Patie Kay

TAB Books
Division of McGraw-Hill, Inc.
Blue Ridge Summit, PA 17294-0850

FIRST EDITION
SECOND PRINTING

Library of Congress Cataloging-in-Publication Data

Williams, Gene B.
   Compact disc players / by Gene B. Williams.
      p. cm.
   Includes index.
   ISBN 0-8306-4179-3 (P)
   1. Compact discs.   I. Title
TK7882.C56W55   1992   92-16897
621.389′32--dc20   CIP

Acquisitions editor: Roland Phelps
Editorial team: Melanie Brewer, Editor
           Stacey R. Spurlock, Indexer
Design team: Jaclyn J. Boone, Designer
          Brian Allison, Associate Designer
Production team: Katherine G. Brown, Director
             Wanda S. Ditch, Layout
             Susan E. Hansford, Typesetting
             Ollie Harmon, Typesetting
             Linda L. King, Proofreading
             Kelly S. Christman, Proofreading
Cover design: Lori E. Schlosser
Cover illustration: Denny Bond, East Petersburg, Pa.
Cartoon caricature: Michael Malle, Pittsburgh, Pa.   ATS

The All Thumbs Guarantee

TAB Books/McGraw-Hill guarantees that you will be able to follow every step of each project in this book, from beginning to end, or you will receive your money back. If you are unable to follow the All Thumbs steps, return this book, your store receipt, and a brief explanation to:

All Thumbs
P.O. Box 581
Blue Ridge Summit, Pa 17214-9998

About the Binding

This and every All Thumbs book has a special lay-flat binding. To take full advantage of this binding, open the book to any page and run your finger along the spine, pressing down as you do so; the book will stay open at the page you've selected.

The lay-flat binding is designed to withstand constant use. Unlike regular book bindings, the spine will not weaken or crack when you press down on the spine to keep the book open.

Dedication

To Nicker and Emily

Acknowledgments

The spirit of this "All Thumbs" series is shown in a six-year-old boy who sits in front of Daddy's Big Computer System like a skilled, two-handed typist. He has no trouble because he expects none. For him, he expects it to work, therefore it does.

Danny is a continuation. Ol' dad here couldn't keep his hands off the knobs, buttons, and switches. My father, Gorden, saw it as an opportunity, not a problem. He built me a "switch box." I don't remember it all that well, but the fascination remains, and is now growing in my son.

The creation of a project and of a skill is a series of events. I didn't just sit down one afternoon and decide to become a technical writer. There was encouragement from my parents to explore any avenue that curiosity stirred. There were also many teachers, such as Melvin Hoke. It builds over the years.

It's now passed to another generation and to all of my readers. If you find yourself frustrated or afraid, think of that six-year-old boy.

Contents

Preface

A collection of books about do-it-yourself home repair and improvement, the All Thumbs series was created not for the skilled jack-of-all-trades, but for the average homeowner. If your familiarity with the various systems in the home is minimal, or your budget doesn't keep pace with today's climbing costs, this series is tailor-made for you.

Not all that many years ago, recordings were made on wax cylinders. These were highly sensitive to heat and didn't last long. Along came plastic records. Both durability and fidelity were increased, but these first records are now antique collector's items. Vinyl-based LPs (long-playing records) are heading in that same direction. They are being replaced by cassette tapes and by CDs. With CDs fast becoming the standard, more and more homes now have CD players.

The main reason for the incredible popularity is the virtually perfect sound reproduction. Another is that the CD isn't prone to damage the way an LP is. With an LP, each time it is played, there is some slight (and additive) damage. With a CD, you can play it thousands of times with absolutely no change to the sound quality. However, the CD isn't as invulnerable as some salespeople might lead you to believe. There are certain steps you must take to protect them.

Although it is "high-tech," the player is very simple in operation. There are very few things that can go wrong with it. Of those things, most can be cured-and prevented from happening—by following some simple steps.

The All Thumbs series saves you time and money by showing you how to make most common repairs yourself. The guides cover topics such as home wiring; plumbing; painting, stenciling, and wallpapering; repairing major appliances; home energy savings; and VCRs, to name a few. Copiously illustrated, each book details the procedures in an easy-to-follow, step-by-step format, making many repairs and home improvements well within the ability of nearly any homeowner.

Introduction

Not that many years ago "high-tech home entertainment" meant gathering around a very large cabinet and listening to scratchy radio broadcasts. When television came along, radio decreased in popularity. Then along came the invention of the transistor. Suddenly it was possible to carry a radio in your pocket.

Audio quality continued to increase. Units not that long ago boasted a distortion level of less than 5 percent. Today it's not difficult to find home stereos with distortion levels of just a tiny fraction of a percent.

Meanwhile the quality of records increased. This was due in part to better manufacturing methods, but also to better recording methods. Still, even the best recording suffers from something called "tape hiss." This same problem occurs with video recordings as well.

While all this was happening, the invention of the integrated circuit made it possible to build electronic equipment that was even smaller than the transistorized units. One of the areas that advanced was computers. A decade ago it was somewhat unusual to find someone with a computer in their home. Today having a home computer is quite common.

A regular tape recorder is analog, which means that the recording is made as a line of varying electronic signals. The computer is binary, which means that it uses pulses that are either on or off (represented by the numbers 1 and 0). Recording data digitally is extraordinarily efficient. The device that reads the recorded signals has only to read on or off, and not a signal that varies across a wide range. Noise is virtually nonexistent. And more data can be stored in a smaller place. All this makes it perfect to use for information storage with computers.

In the mid-1980s Philips of Holland applied this technology to video. They and Sony of Japan developed a method by which movies could be recorded digitally on a disk and then read back by focusing a laser on the disk. It was called LaserVision. It promised almost completely distortion-free images and sound that would not degrade over time, and it kept the promise!

It didn't take long for this new concept to be used for audio recordings—and the first CD was born. In the few years since then, compact disks (CDs) have almost wiped out the LP (record) market. The recording quality of a CD is superior; the disk doesn't wear so you can play it over and over without any loss of quality; and the disk is less effected by the environment (dust, etc.) than are records. It's no wonder that CDs have become so popular.

However, contrary to what many salespeople have claimed, neither the players nor the disks are infallible. Many people purchase and install a player, then invest in a collection of CDs, only to find themselves plagued with troubles.

As with many things, the owner may feel so intimidated at the idea of even operating the machine that the idea of getting inside to take care of it is thought to be absurd. After all, the player uses a laser!

This is true. It's equally true that the very technology that makes the CD and the CD player possible also makes it possible for you to take care of it with a minimum of effort, knowledge, tools, or technical background.

What might surprise you is that the professional technician usually can't do much more than you can do for yourself. It might go faster for the trained technician, but you can accomplish almost everything he or she can.

Follow the maintenance steps provided in this book and the number of malfunctions will be greatly reduced. You'll face fewer repairs and the repairs you do encounter will be less serious repairs, many of which you will be able to handle yourself. Also your player and disks will last longer.

Chapter 1 explains the importance of safety. A screwdriver and your fingers are the most important tools you'll need. Other tools that might come in handy are needle-nose pliers, regular pliers, nut driver set, and cleaning materials. The most complicated tool you would use is a VOM (volt-ohmmeter), and this is an optional tool. All these tools and how to use them will be described in chapter 2. A complete appendix is dedicated to the VOM and how to use it.

In chapter 3 you will learn the basics of how a CD player works. This chapter will give you all the technical background you need to handle troubleshooting and repairs. How to go about troubleshooting is detailed in chapter 4. This includes instructions on how you can make your own test disc that will be useful both in diagnosing problems and in selecting a player.

With this essential but simple background, you're ready to open the CD player. This is easier than you might suspect. Chapter 5 tells you exactly how to get inside and describes the basic cleaning and maintenance steps that will solve a large number of common problems, and prevent others.

Chapter 7 details some of the simple checks and repairs you can make. You'll learn how to examine both the discs and the player for damage that could be causing the problem. You'll also learn how to check the player for things such as worn, stretched, or broken belts.

The discs themselves are covered in chapter 6. With this information you can take care of your discs so they'll last longer and give fewer problems.

Most CD player owners need nothing more than to connect the player to the stereo, and the stereo to the speakers. This is generally no more complicated than plugging in the various cables and wires into existing connectors. Other times the connection of equipment will involve using older stereo equipment that does not have a CD input. Or you might want to locate and wire some remote speakers so you can enjoy the music in a place more distant from the stereo. This information is covered in chapter 8.

CD players have become extremely popular in homes. There is also a growing popularity for more portable players. These include those in automobiles and those you can carry around with you. These portable units are essentially the same as the home units, but there are some interesting differences. Chapter 9 shows you what these differences are, and how you can better take care of these units.

Some of the tests described in this guide require a VOM (volt-ohmmeter). If you have never used a VOM before, don't worry. A special appendix is included to show you exactly what to do and how to do it.

CHAPTER ONE

Safety

Safety is essential for you to know and practice. It is important for everyone, especially for beginners who might not know all of the potential dangers. Most of the circuits in the CD player present no danger to you. However, the power coming out of the wall outlet and going into the power supply can measure 120 lethal volts.

Getting a jolt from the incoming 120 volts ac (120 Vac) is more than just unpleasant; it can be fatal. Studies have shown that it takes very little current to kill. Even a small amount of current can paralyze your muscles and you won't be able to let go. Just a fraction more and your heart muscle can become paralyzed.

There is almost nothing mechanical in the CD player that can harm you. About the most that can happen is you'll get a pinched finger. There is however a greater threat to the CD player. Some of the parts can be easily damaged. Touching the wrong place can make a short circuit and cause a critical circuit to go up in smoke. Moving parts can get broken, bent, damaged, or knocked out of alignment. If any of these things happen, the CD player will not work correctly. If something goes wrong, more damage could result because all the parts (including the disc itself) work together.

The CD player brings with it another danger, namely the laser. Although this laser is a very low-powered device, and theoretically cannot cause harm, it's possible. If the beam hits the retina of your eye you probably won't feel anything; however, you can simply and quickly go blind.

Now that you are sufficiently frightened, relax. As long as you are careful, take your time, and follow the rules of safety and common sense, you won't get into trouble.

Before beginning any work inside the CD player, remove all jewelry, especially jewelry that dangles. A lot of jewelry is made of metal, which is electrically conductive. You might short a circuit or get shocked if a ring or necklace comes in contact with something it shouldn't.

Every time you work on your CD player, exercise the following steps.

Step 1-1. Unplugging your unit.
For safety's sake, unplug the CD player before opening the cabinet. Doing this might mean having to reset the clock and other controls, but you'll be certain that you can't possibly get shocked, and can't accidentally cause a short circuit that can damage the CD player. The correct way to unplug any appliance or device is to grasp the plug. Never pull on the cord; this can cause the cord to pull loose from the plug.

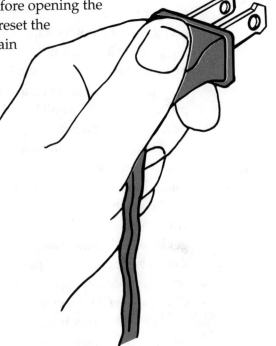

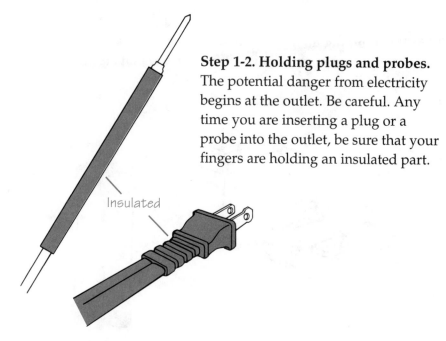

Step 1-2. Holding plugs and probes.
The potential danger from electricity begins at the outlet. Be careful. Any time you are inserting a plug or a probe into the outlet, be sure that your fingers are holding an insulated part.

Insulated

Step 1-3. Locating the power supply.
If power must be on, be very careful wherever electricity comes into the CD player, such as around the power supply. The power supply is usually located in a rear corner. Look to see where the power cord enters the machine and you'll find the power supply.

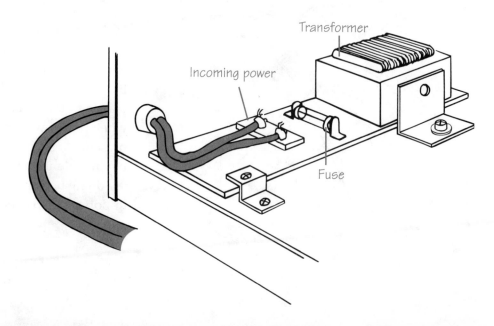

Transformer

Incoming power

Fuse

Step 1-4. Avoiding dangerous circuits.

Be careful around fuses. Almost all fuses in CD players are used to protect the CD player from 120 volts ac. These fuses are located near the power supply. See step 1-3.

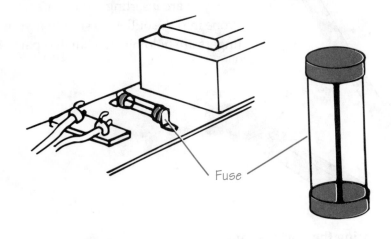

Fuse

Step 1-5. Probing inside your CD player.

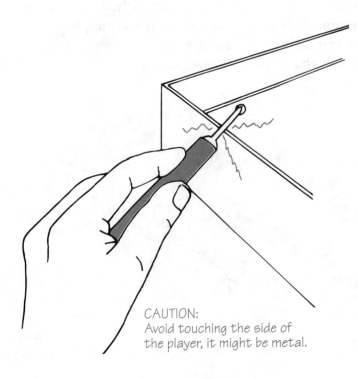

CAUTION:
Avoid touching the side of the player, it might be metal.

Metal probes and tools can cause short circuits and other damage. This is not a danger if you've unplugged the CD player, but there are times when power will have to be present. At such times, paying attention to what you are doing becomes more important than ever.

Step 1-6. Avoiding contact with the laser head assembly.

When working inside the CD player, move slowly and carefully. It's easy to cause damage to the delicate parts. Be especially careful around the laser head assembly, and never touch it with your bare fingers. This can cause permanent damage. So can excessive pressure. Alignment of the assembly is critical. Also be aware that the laser represents a severe danger to your eyes. Unless absolutely essential, never have the player on and powered while working inside.

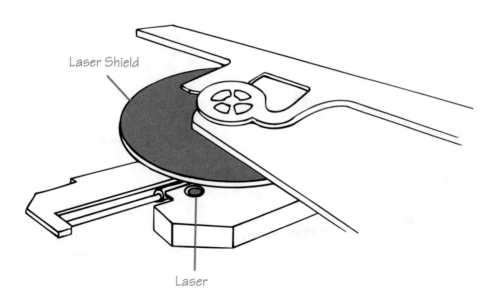

Laser Shield

Laser

CHAPTER TWO

Tools

Probably the tools you'll need to troubleshoot and repair your CD player can be found around the house. None of the tools and materials you'll need are costly. The most expensive is the optional VOM; a unit costing about $10 to $20 will be sufficient. Avoid buying poor-quality tools. A cheap screwdriver might do the job just as well as an expensive one; however, it also can cause you considerable trouble. There are reasons why a cheap tool is cheap. The materials used are of lower standards. The metal can bend and break, or the coating can flake off and fall inside the machine where it can cause considerable damage.

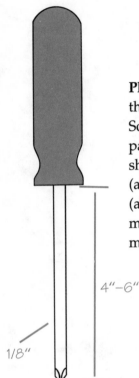

4"–6"

1/8"

Phillips screwdrivers   Invariably, the cabinet of the CD player will be held by Phillips-type screws. So will be most internal shields and many other parts. The head of a Phillips screwdriver is in the shape of an x. Get one with a medium-sized head (about 1/4 inch) and one with a small-sized head (about 1/8 inch). The shaft length isn't critical, but most people find a length of 4 to 6 inches to be the most convenient and versatile.

Blade-type screwdriver   Occasionally you will have to remove a standard slotted screw. A blade screwdriver does this. It is critical that the blade of the screwdriver exactly fits the slot of the screw. Several sizes might be needed. You can begin with a medium (about 1/4 inch) and a small (1/8 inch). Shaft length is the same as with the Phillips screwdriver. It's important that the screwdriver fits the screw, both for the length of the slot and for the width. The same is true of the Phillips screw and screwdriver. The head should fit the slot.

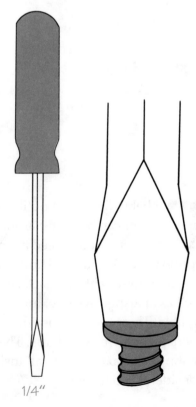

1/4"

Needle-nose pliers Needle-nose pliers are good for light gripping, parts retrieval, and for a variety of other tasks. For the sake of safety, get pliers with insulated handles.

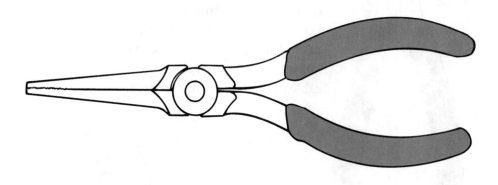

Standard pliers This tool is a versatile gripping device that comes in hand for a variety of tasks. You will rarely need them inside the player, but they can be used for other gripping jobs. They also can be used for crimping some connectors onto the wire. As with the needle-nose pliers, it's best if the handles are insulated.

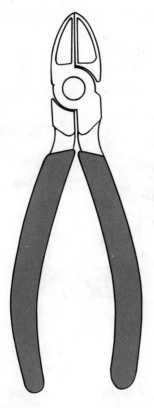

Wire cutters   If you intend to do any kind of wiring or cabling, a pair of wire cutters is essential. They should be large enough to cut through the wire or cable easily. The largest cable you'll have to cut is an audio cable of about 3/8 inch in diameter.

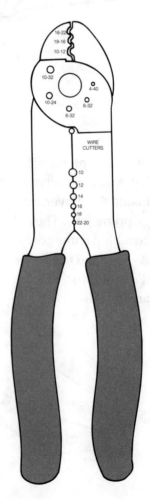

Combination cutter/stripper   A combination tool serves the purpose of both cutting and stripping a wire. It has a number of holes and notches for the different wire sizes, and a small blade. The blade is for actually cutting the wire. The holes and notches strip off the insulation without nicking the conductor inside. When using this tool it is important to use the right stripping hole for the wire. Some will also have built-in crimpers for attaching connectors to the wire/cable.

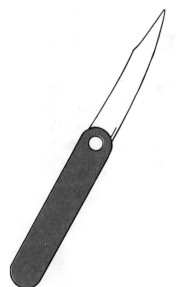

Knife   A sharp knife is a valuable tool to have around. It is almost essential if you are to work with audio cable, which is larger than any hole in a wire stripper. Here the knife is used to cut through the layers of insulation one at a time.

Isopropyl alcohol   This is the standard cleaning fluid. It's inexpensive and relatively safe to use. For a CD player, be sure to get technical grade isopropyl alcohol, with a purity of at least 95 percent, with 99 percent purity being preferred. *Caution!* Do not use alcohol on any rubber parts.

Isopropyl alcohol

99% pure

Special cleaning fluids   These fluids are more expensive than alcohol; however, they are often better cleaners. Get a cleaner that leaves no residue and is safe for the rubber parts. Usually the label will tell you.

Compressed air   You can buy cans of compressed air in camera shops. You can use compressed air to clean hard-to-reach places in the CD player or use it on the discs.

Cleaning swabs   The swabs used must be of the appropriate material. Those with threads, like cotton swabs, are just barely tolerable for general cleaning inside. Instead use the foam swabs, available in most electronics and video supply stores.

CD Disc Cleaning Unit   CDs collect dust and other contaminants that can cause the player to "skip." The discs can be cleaned by hand or by disc cleaning units. If you buy a disc cleaning unit, be sure that it cleans from the center to the edge and back to the center again. It should not clean in circles.

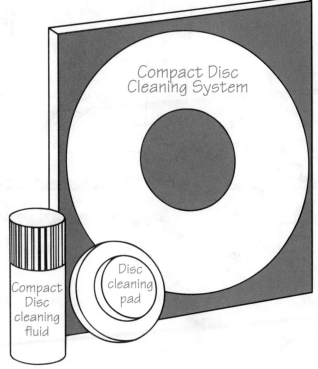

Volt-ohmmeter A volt-ohmmeter, also called a VOM or multimeter, is used to measure voltage and resistance. It is an invaluable tool to have around the house because you can make power tests, continuity tests, and other tests. Most of the tests you'll be making will not require high accuracy, so an inexpensive VOM works fine. (See the appendix.)

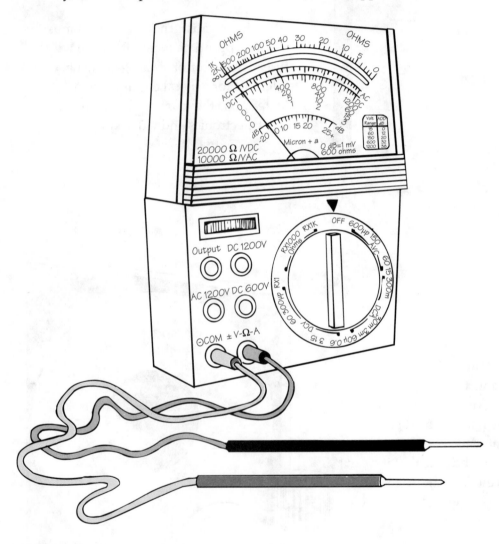

This final section covers the various tools you might or might not need. You don't have to buy any of these tools until the need arises.

Many of the things you'll need can be found around the house. A muffin tin or paper cups can be used to hold removed screws or other parts.

Nut driver   Occasionally there will be parts that are held by bolts or screws with bolt (hex) heads. Although wrenches can sometimes be used, the easiest way usually is to use a nut driver. This tool is much like a combination of a screwdriver and a socket. They can be purchased individually but are more often found in sets. This is a tool set you don't have to buy until the need arises.

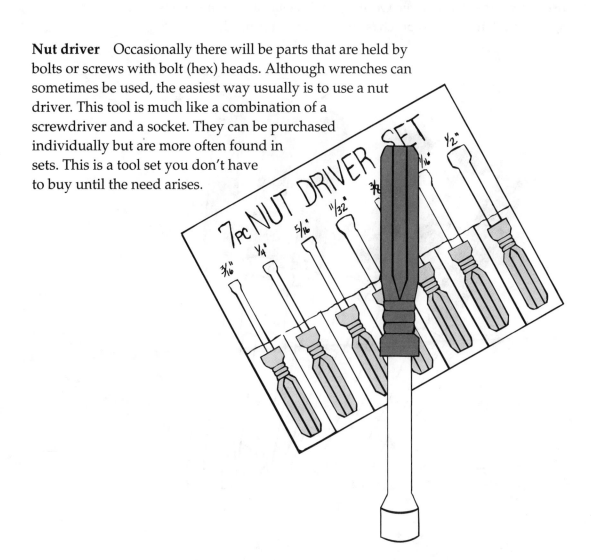

Jeweler's screwdrivers Sometimes you will need to remove or work with a screw with a very small head. At such times you might need to use a jeweler's screwdriver. Once again these usually come in sets, and again you don't have to purchase the set until it is needed.

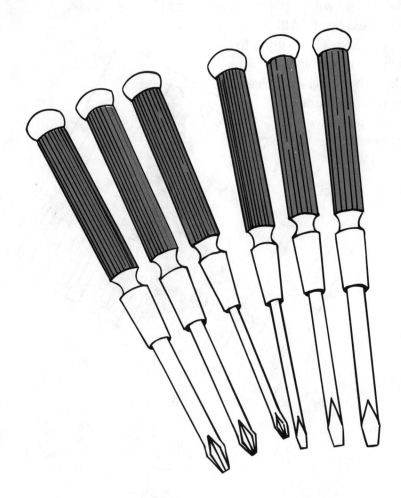

CHAPTER THREE

Operating Your CD Player

Imagine trying to fix a car without having any idea what makes it work. You generally don't need this understanding if you will be merely operating the device or machine (although it can help), but when it comes to troubleshooting and repairing, the knowledge is essential.

Before this frightens you, your goal isn't to learn how to design and engineer a CD player. All you need to know are the basics of how it operates. For example, the programming of the CD player is operated by one or more electronic chips (integrated circuits) and related circuitry. You do not need to know how to design such a circuit to be able to push the buttons that set the programming. And you don't need to know how to design a power supply to understand what it does, or to be able to make the simple tests to see if it is working.

Learning how a CD player works isn't difficult. Your greatest enemy is "high-tech intimidation." Being cautious and recognizing your honest limitations is wise. Being intimidated to the point that you feel totally incompetent isn't necessary.

The front panel controls of CD players both differ and are much the same from model to model. The instruction manual for your specific unit is the best guide for that unit. Notice the similarities, and the differences, between this unit and yours.

Many of the controls, such as Play and Stop, are self-explanatory. The Pause button temporarily stops the play. Depending on the player, play can be resumed either by pressing Pause again or by pressing Play. For both Play and Pause an LED indicator will light.

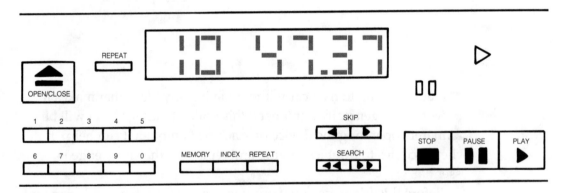

Front panel controls

Step 3-1. Loading the disc.

To play a disc you have to load it, which means you have to open the drawer. The button to do this is usually next to or very near the drawer. The same button is used to close the drawer and complete the loading.

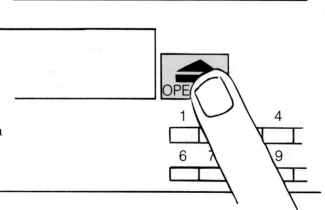

Step 3-2. Checking the loading indicator.

If the disc isn't loaded correctly, it can't be played. Some CD players have an indicator such as "Load" or "Disc" if there is no disc in the machine, or if the one inside isn't loaded properly.

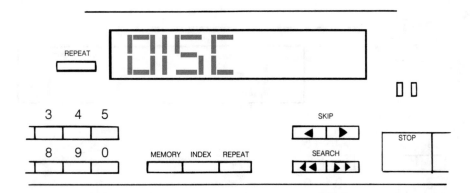

Step 3-3. Scanning a disc.

The Forward and Reverse Search buttons, often shown with double arrows, are used to scan through the recording. You can jump from track to track forward or backward using the Skip buttons.

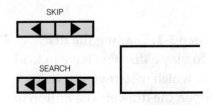

Step 3-4. Programming your player.

If you wish to listen to the tracks in a certain order, you can program the player. This is usually done with a 10-digit keypad. When you press the number of the track, the Memory button "enters" that number into the player's memory. To program more than one track, simply repeat the process. The index marks are recorded on the disc. Pressing "index" causes the player to search for the next mark.

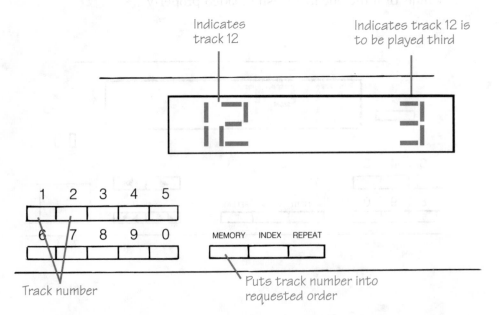

Indicates track 12

Indicates track 12 is to be played third

Track number

Puts track number into requested order

Step 3-5. Using the Repeat key.

Your selections, or the entire disc if the player wasn't programmed, can be repeated using the Repeat key. Some units also have an Index control that allows you to search for prerecording indexing spots that are on some CDs. The index marks are recorded on the disc Pressing "index" causes the player to search for the next mark.

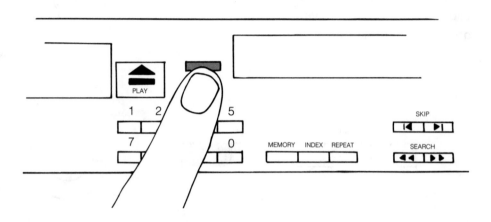

Step 3-6.
Checking your display.

The player will have at least one display area. This is used to give you information such as the track number and playing time, to allow programming and so forth. The display area also might be switchable to show different kinds of information. More information on connecting the CD player to the stereo and troubleshooting this part of the system is covered in chapter 8.

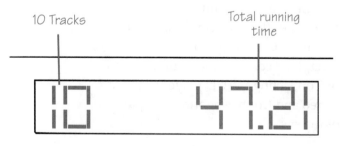

10 Tracks

Total running time

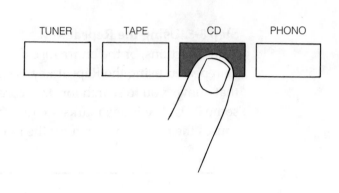

Step 3-7. Connecting your CD player to your stereo.
Most modern stereo units have a button designed to accept input from a CD player. Other stereos, especially older ones, have an Aux button that can be used.

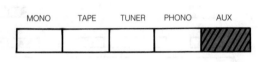

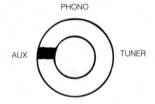

The CD player is connected with two cables (left track and right track) that use RCA-type phone plugs. Chapter 8 contains more information on connecting the CD player to the stereo and troubleshooting this part of the system.

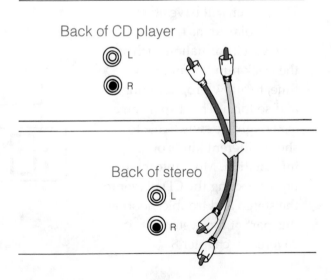

Step 3-8. Examining the disc.

The disc is made of optical plastic that has a layer of reflective aluminum on which the recording is held. This reflective layer is 0.1cm thick. The disc is 12 cm (about 4.7 inches) across, with a center hole of 15 mm. The outer and inner edges are clear. The rest of the disc is used to hold the recording and other information needed by the player. (Actually only 32.7 percent of the total recorded space is used for audio.)

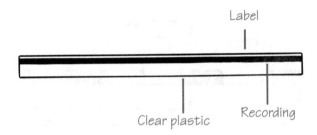

Label

Clear plastic   Recording

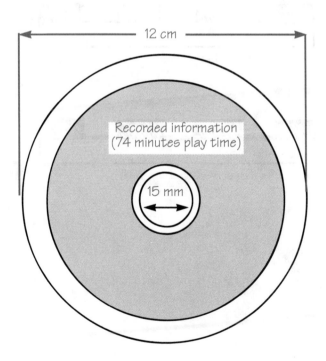

12 cm

Recorded information
(74 minutes play time)

15 mm

When a CD is made, a laser is shined on a light sensitive
surface. This surface is then processed to remove the exposed spots,
and then silvering is applied. This makes a "metal master" from which
"stampers" are made. These are then used to make the copies you buy.

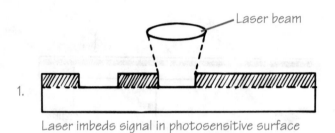

1.

Laser imbeds signal in photosensitive surface

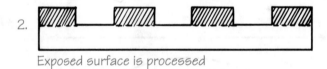

2.

Exposed surface is processed

3.

Reflection material added

The recording consists of highly reflective "lands" and low reflective "pits." As the laser scans the disc, the transition from a land to a pit, or from a pit to a land, causes a *binary 1* to occur. This is like turning on a switch. Everywhere else is a *binary 0* (like turning a switch off). This creates a binary (digital) coding which the player processes and turns into the music you hear. How many binary 1s and 0s are "read" is dependent on the size of the lands and pits. Notice in the illustration that the numeral 1 starts at the exact edge between the land and pit. The number of zeros used between the ones is not important.

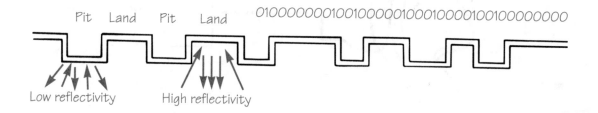

Pit   Land   Pit   Land   0100000000100100000100010000100100000000

Low reflectivity   High reflectivity

All of this works because of changing analog signals into digital signals and back into analog signals. The term analog means that the signal is constantly varying. For recording this has to be changed into the on/off digital coding, and later during play it must be changed back into the analog signal of the stereo speakers.

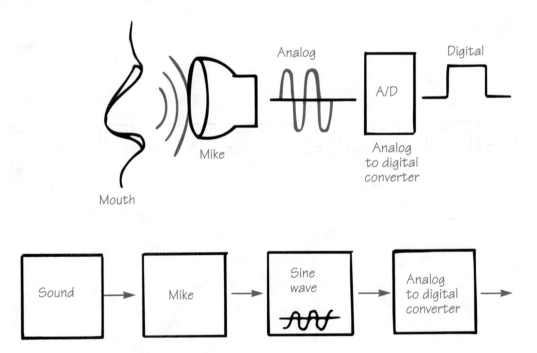

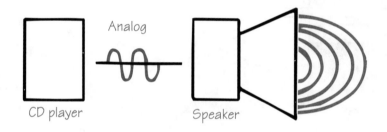

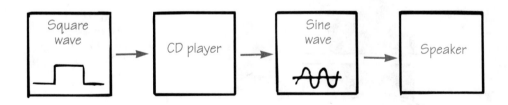

Just as a laser is used to create the recording, a laser is used to read it. The process is the same. The transition between a land and a pit causes a binary 1 (on), while all other areas are a binary 0 (off). The beam is "processed" by the parts of the optical system. It strikes the disk, "reads" the recording and is then reflected back to a photo diode detector.

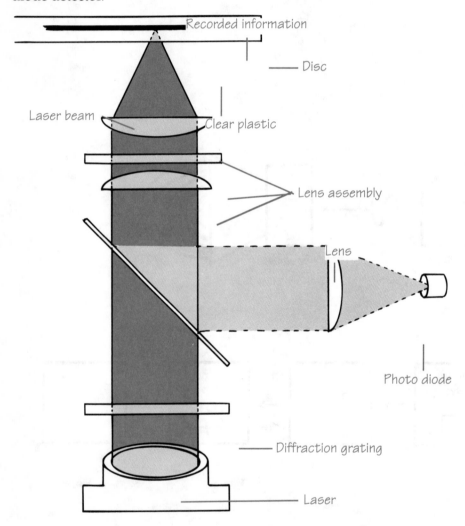

Recorded information

Disc

Laser beam

Clear plastic

Lens assembly

Lens

Photo diode

Diffraction grating

Laser

A "3-beam" player operates in much the same way except that the laser beam is split into three beams. The two smaller sub-beams are used to aid in accurate tracking.

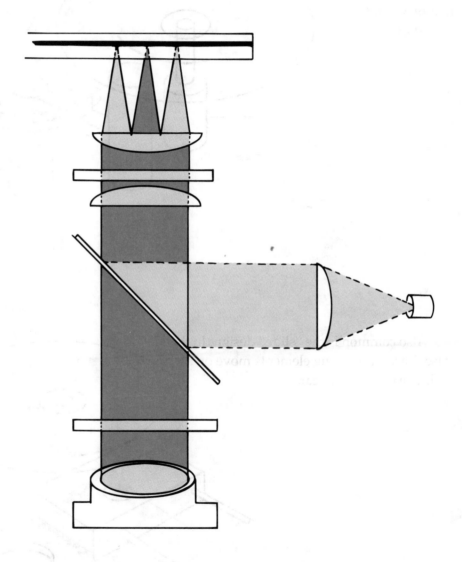

A 1-beam player might use a "swing arm" mechanism to move the beam over the disc. With this design the laser is beneath. It's motion is similar to that of a standard record player.

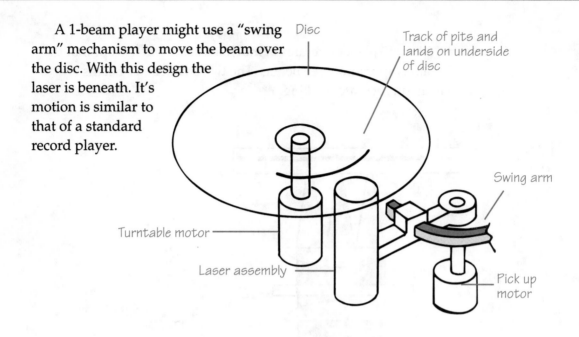

Disc

Track of pits and lands on underside of disc

Swing arm

Turntable motor

Laser assembly

Pick up motor

Also common is the "slide" design. In this case the laser focusing elements move on a rail. The motion is linear.

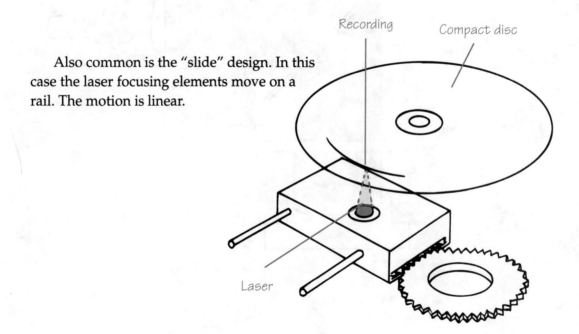

Recording

Compact disc

Laser

One reason that CDs are less prone to problems from spots, marks, and scratches than a record is that the laser works by critical focus. It focuses on the reflective aluminum. Small mars on the surface of the disc are out of focus.

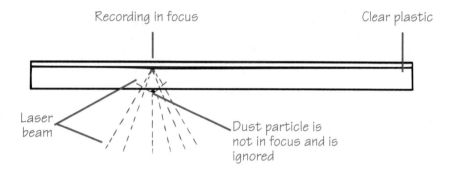

Recording in focus   Clear plastic

Laser beam

Dust particle is not in focus and is ignored

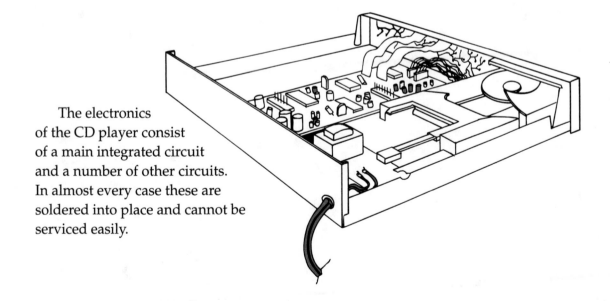

The electronics of the CD player consist of a main integrated circuit and a number of other circuits. In almost every case these are soldered into place and cannot be serviced easily.

CHAPTER FOUR

Basic Troubleshooting

Troubleshooting is a step-by-step process of elimination. Once you've eliminated all the places where the problem is not, you find out where it is. At times the procedures for solving common problems require tests inside the CD player with the power on. *Be careful!* (Refer to chapter 1.) If you don't feel competent to do something that even *might* be dangerous to you or to the player, don't do it! Call a professional technician.

The process always begins with the simple and progresses to the more complex. Start by looking for the obvious. Where you begin is determined by the general symptoms. For example, if the machine is completely dead, trying a different disc in the player won't help. Likewise, if you obviously have power to the unit, checking the house fuses or circuit breakers is a waste of time.

Once you've determined what is going wrong, you can begin to find out why the player is malfunctioning and what to do about it. A troubleshooting list, such as the one in the owner's manual or the one at the beginning of this chapter, can help.

The CD system consists of three parts: the player itself, the discs it plays, and the stereo. Sometimes what seems to be a serious problem with the player is actually nothing more than a bad disc or perhaps a loose connection between the player and the stereo.

Tools & Materials
- ❏ Voltohm-milliameter (VOM)
- ❏ CD disc
- ❏ 1/32-inch black matte artist's tape or a fine-point permanent marker
- ❏ Cloth
- ❏ Cleaning fluid

TROUBLESHOOTING GUIDE

Problem	Possible cause	Solutions
No power	Dead wall outlet.	Check outlet.
	Blown fuse or circuit breaker.	Check or replace.
	Bad power supply.	Check input and output voltage.
	Short circuit.	Check for short/continuity.
Fails to play	Disc not loaded.	Insert disc.
	Disc not properly loaded.	Reload.
	Bad power supply.	
	Stereo malfunction.	Check stereo.
Poor-quality sound	Dirty or damaged disc.	Replace the disc.
	Dirty machine	Clean the player.
	Bad cables or connectors.	Clean or replace them.
Skipping	Dirty or damaged disc.	Replace the disc.
	Dirty machine.	Clean the machine.
	Excessive vibration.	Move player.
Tray does not close	Object in the path.	Clear object.
Noise	Bad cables or connectors.	Clean or replace them.
	Interference.	Move player.
	Warped disc.	Replace disc.

Step 4-1.
Checking the obvious
when nothing happens.
If nothing at all is happening, look to see
if the unit is plugged in. If it is plugged
in, is it turned on? Another possibility is that the outlet is
dead. Test the outlet by plugging something such as a
lamp into it. Don't forget that some outlets are operated
with a wall switch.

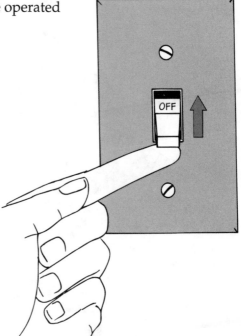

Indicator on
base of VOM

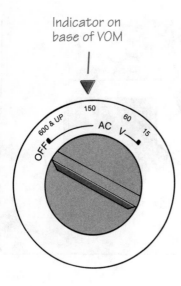

Step 4-2. Using a VOM.

A VOM can be used for a more accurate test for power. Set the dial to read in the 120 volts ac range. Insert the probes into the outlet slots (being careful to hold the probes only by the insulation). Because the wall outlet has ac voltage, it doesn't matter which probe goes in which slot.

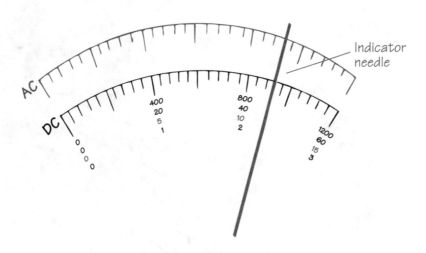

Indicator
needle

Step 4-3.
Checking the fuse or circuit breaker.
Usually you can see if the fuse wire is melted by looking through the "window" of the fuse.

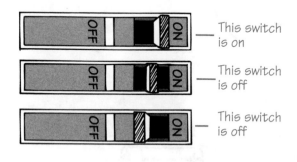

— This switch is on

— This switch is off

— This switch is off

A popped circuit breaker might not be quite so easy to see. Normally the lever will be slightly back, but sometimes this is so slight that it is difficult to see. When in doubt, flip the breaker completely off and back on again.

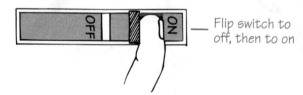

— Flip switch to off, then to on

Step 4-4. Changing the fuse.
If the outlet is good but the player still won't "power up," its own fuse might be blown. You will have to open the cabinet (see chapter 5) to get at the fuse. As with the household fuse, you can usually just look through the glass to see if the fuse wire inside is melted.

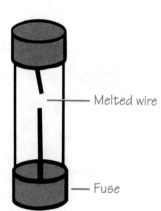

— Melted wire

— Fuse

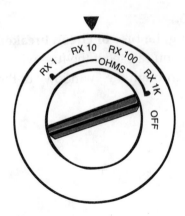

Step 4-5.
Testing the fuse with a VOM.

Sometimes a fuse will look good when it is actually bad. If you suspect this, shut off all power and unplug the player. Remove the fuse from its holder. Set your VOM to read resistance; any range will do. Touch the probes to each end of the fuse. You should get a reading of very nearly zero ohms. If the fuse shows a high resistance, it has "blown" and must be replaced.

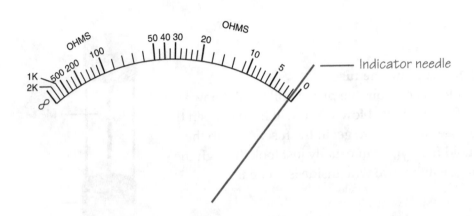

Step 4-6. Testing for power going into the power supply.
The final VOM tests involve the power supply. Be very careful doing
these tests. The unit has to be plugged in, and the player power on.
First, set the dial of the VOM to test for ac in the 120-volt range.

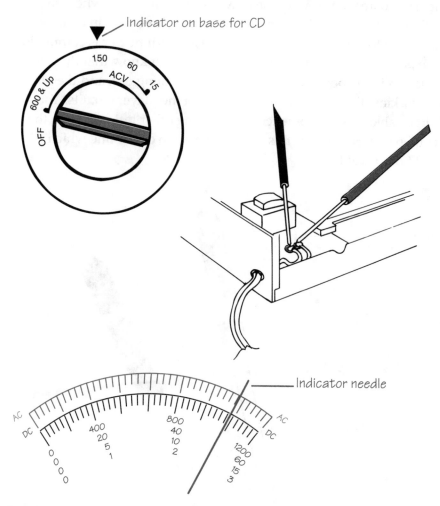

Carefully touch the two probes to the spots where the incoming power
cord is soldered. You can find this by simply looking at where the
power cord enters the machine and following the cord inside. If you
don't read approximately 120 Vac (it won't be exactly 120), no power is
getting to the unit. Either the outlet is dead, the cord is no good, or the
soldered joints are bad.

Step 4-7. Testing for power coming out of the power supply.
If power is getting to the power supply, is it coming out? How you find
out depends on how your own player is built. Usually you have to find
where the wires come out of the power supply and look where they
attach to a circuit board. Set the VOM to read dc voltage in a range
above 12 volts (but not too far above). Basically, if power is coming in
to the power supply but none is coming out, you know that the
problem is in the power supply. If power is coming out, and the player
isn't working, the problem is somewhere in the player circuits. You
might be able to make some tests by locating other test points on the
circuit boards. Sometimes this will allow you to determine which
circuit board is at fault.

Step 4-8.
Making sure the disc is loaded correctly.
If the disc drawer won't open, first check to be sure that the power is
on. If there is power and the drawer won't open, either the motor isn't
functioning or something is jamming the mechanism.
You will have to open the case (see chapter 5) to
examine the mechanism. If the disc loads but will not
play, first check to be sure that it has been inserted
with the label-side up and that the disc is flat and
centered in the tray.

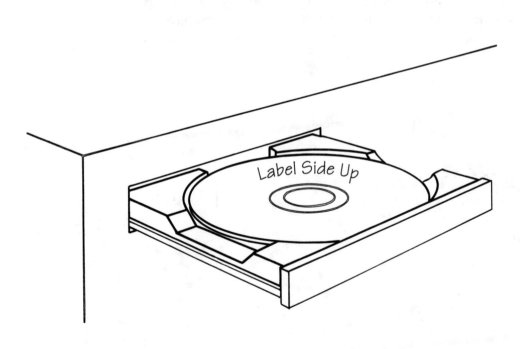

Step 4-9. Examining the disc for damage.

Check the disc itself. Look to see if it is warped, damaged, or dirty. If the disc is damaged, it will have to be replaced. If dirty, you can probably clean it (see chapter 5). Notice that in almost every case even a very dirty disc will play, but poorly. If the disc doesn't play at all it will usually mean that the disc is badly damaged or that something else is wrong.

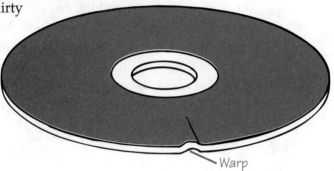

Warp

Playing problems can often be cured by thoroughly cleaning the player (see chapter 5 for more details). If the previous steps haven't cured the problem, before you bring the player to a technician, clean it.

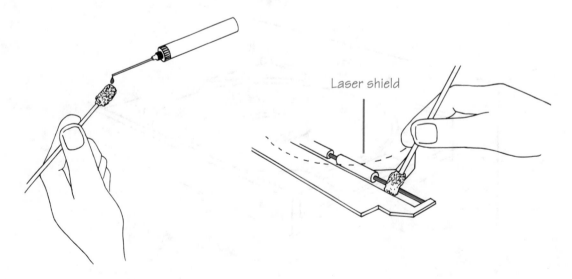

Laser shield

Clean the interior.

Step 4-10. Checking the stereo.

Don't forget that the stereo is a part of the overall system. It could be that the player is operating perfectly and that the problem is with the stereo. Check to be sure that the stereo is working and is properly set. You can verify that the stereo is working by simply setting it to one of the other modes (e.g., set it to play the tuner or turntable).

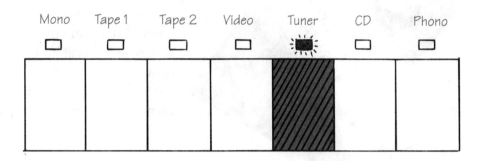

Mono	Tape 1	Tape 2	Video	Tuner	CD	Phono

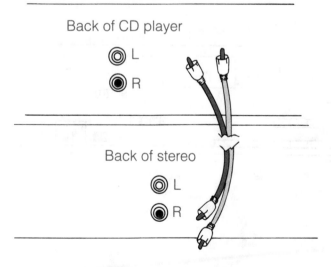

Back of CD player

◎ L
◉ R

Back of stereo

◎ L
◉ R

Step 4-11. Examining cables and connectors.

If there is no sound, yet the stereo is definitely on and functioning, check the cables and connectors. If they are connected correctly, you might have to remove the cables and test them. Chapter 8 shows you how.

Step 4-12.
Checking for programming errors.
If a programmed playback doesn't work, chances are that you did something wrong in setting the controls. Look over the various controls for this, and study the owner's manual for your particular machine.

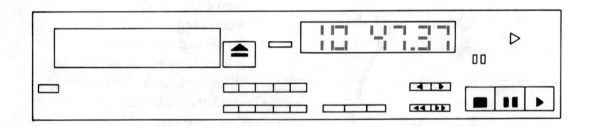

Step 4-13. Making a test disc.

Having a test disc can help both in diagnosis and for testing a CD player before purchase. For this you should use a disc that is in good condition but which you don't need. Use 1/32-inch black matte artist's tape or a fine-point permanent marker (such as one used to mark on photographic paper) to make test stripes on the disc. Both can leave a permanent deposit on the disc, which is why you should use a disc that isn't wanted. Draw at least four lines on the clear side of the disc, 90 degrees apart. The laser beam goes through the clear side of the disc. The player has error correction, so any "skips" on the disc can be detected and replaced electronically without hearing a flaw in the recording. The stripes on the test disc serve as blocks in the recording enabling you to check how well the error correction in your player is working. A player in perfect condition should be able to play a test disc with as many as eight stripes. Any CD player that cannot play such a test disc could be having serious problems.

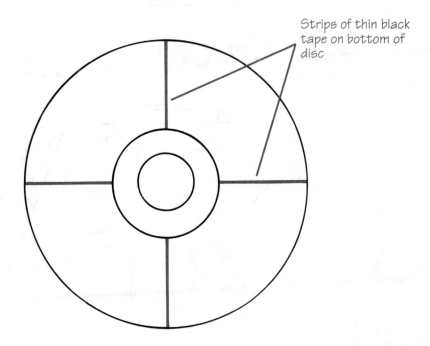

Strips of thin black tape on bottom of disc

Step 4-14.
Checking the remote control.
These days almost every player comes with a wireless remote control. Some use ultrasonics, but most operate using infrared signals. (Both are invisible and perfectly safe.) Become familiar with the controls, how they operate, and what they do. For this refer to the owner's manual. The signal from a remote control can be blocked if something is between the remote control and the player. Excessive distance between the two might also prevent operation.

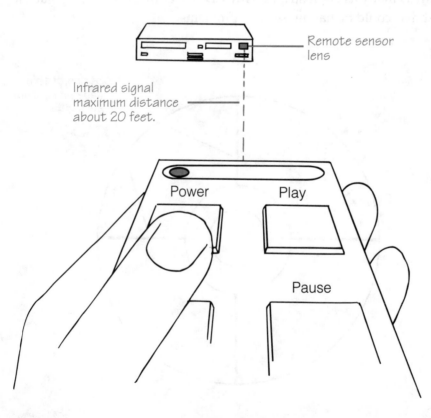

Remote sensor lens

Infrared signal maximum distance about 20 feet.

Step 4-15.
Changing worn-out batteries in your remote control.
The most common cause of remote control
failure, including intermittent
operation, is a worn (or
wearing) battery. Open the
battery compartment and
replace the battery (or batteries).
Pay close attention to the polarity
(the + and − labels). With single-cell batteries
the positive (+) side is the post; the negative (−) is
the flat side.

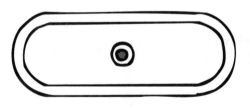

Step 4-16. Cleaning the lenses.
In rare cases, the lens of the remote control
unit or the receiving lens on the CD player
might be so dirty that the signals are partially
blocked. Clean the lenses with a clean, soft
cloth and a cleaning fluid safe for plastic.

Step 4-17. Testing the stereo.

Don't assume that an apparent malfunction is in the player. It is possible that the player is working fine and that the problem is in the stereo. Begin by examining the connectors on both the CD player and on the stereo. Are the cables connected properly?

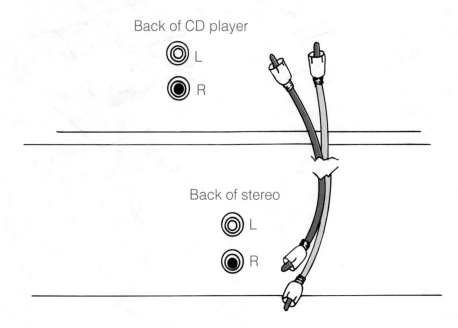

Back of CD player

L

R

Back of stereo

L

R

Step 4-18. Testing the connectors.

It is possible that a connector is bad, especially if either unit has been moved often. An easy test is to wiggle the cable in its connector. If sound comes in and out, either the connector is bad or the cable end is bad. To find out, replace the cable with one that you know is in working condition. If you don't have a replacement cable to test it with, the testing process with a VOM is described and illustrated in the appendix.

Step 4-19. Testing the connector for continuity with a VOM.
If a connector is suspected, it can be tested easily with the VOM. To do this, open the cabinet and find where the connector passes through the rear wall of the player. Set the VOM to read ohms in any scale. With the cable disconnected, touch one probe to the center conductor inside and outside the player. It is best to probe the inside at the spot where the connector is attached to the circuit board. Next, touch the probe to the outer conductor on each side. In both cases, the reading on the VOM should be zero ohms. If it shows infinite ohms or a high reading, there is a break in the conductor and the connector must be repaired or replaced.

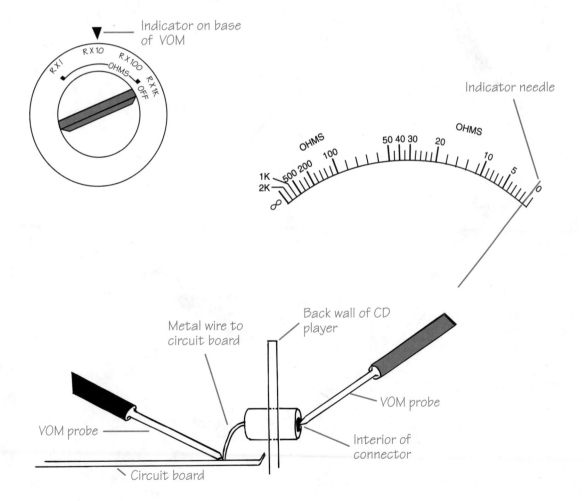

Step 4-20. Testing the connector for a short circuit with a VOM.
It is unlikely but possible that the connector has developed a short. To
test for this, have the VOM set to read ohms in any scale. Touch one
probe to the center conductor and the other to the outer shell. The
reading should be infinite ohms. If it reads zero or low ohms, the
connector has a short and must be replaced.

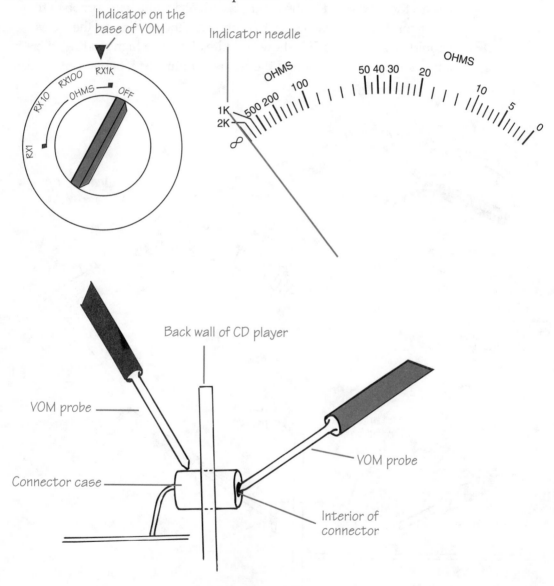

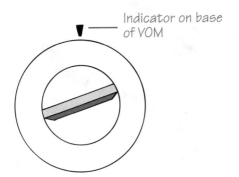

Indicator on base of VOM

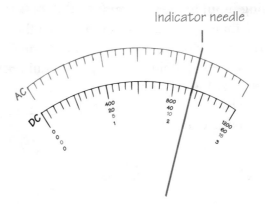

Indicator needle

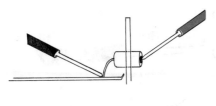

L
R

Step 4-21.

Testing the CD player and stereo output.
It's easy to test the CD player for output. The output should be in the 1–2 volt range. Set your VOM to read ac volts in this range. Disconnect the cables. Touch the VOM probes to the connectors, one at a time, with one probe touching the center conductor and the other probe touching the outer shell. With a CD playing in the player, you should get a reading in the range mentioned. If you don't get that reading, either the connector is bad or the player itself needs to be serviced by a professional. Likewise, when you probe the stereo output (to the speakers) you should get this same reading. If you don't get that reading, either the connector is bad or the stereo needs to be serviced by a professional.

Step 4-22.

Testing input to the speakers.

If everything seems fine, it could be that the speaker is bad, or the speaker wire is bad. You can determine this quickly by probing at the speaker unit. Set the VOM in the 1–2 volt ac range. If the speaker has screw-type terminals, you can probe directly.

If the speaker uses an RCA jack, unplug the cable and probe the cable itself. Again the reading should be within the range. If the stereo output at its connector is correct, but you have no reading at the speaker, the speaker cable is bad. If you get the correct reading, the speaker is probably bad.

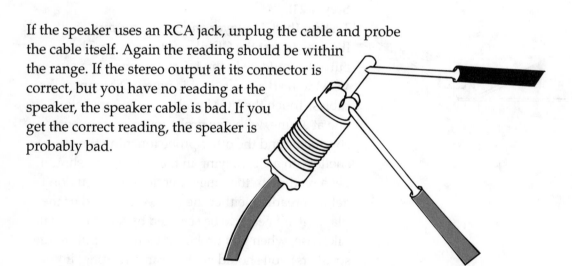

Step 4-23. Checking the speaker polarity.
If you are getting sound at the speakers but it is of poor quality, it is
possible that the polarity is wrong. The signals
being sent to the speakers has a + and –. These
signals must match on both sides. When using
RCA-type connectors, polarity is assured. If the
speakers use two-lead wires, it's easy to have
the polarity reversed. Usually the terminals and
the wires are marked in some way. The terminals
might have a + and –, or they might be color coded
black and red. The wire might have the conductors of
different colors (with gold and silver being common,
or sometimes with the insulation of one conductor
having a stripe).

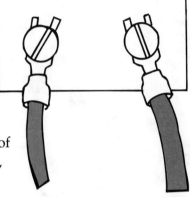

CHAPTER FIVE

Maintenance

Mechanical things have a common enemy—dirt. If a machine is allowed to get dirty and stay dirty, it won't operate correctly. It could stop working entirely or might suffer permanent damage. When they are kept clean, they work better, last longer, and have fewer problems.

Cleaning is the major part of preventive maintenance, and is often the cure for malfunctions. For example, the most common problem with CD players is skipping (when the music hops and jumps). The cause is almost invariably either a dirty disc or a dirty rail. The cure in both cases is proper cleaning.

Tools & Materials

- ❏ Isopropyl alcohol, or liquid cleaning solvent
- ❏ Spray cleaner (nonresidue)—for small connectors
- ❏ Canned compressed air
- ❏ Swabs
- ❏ Lint-free cloth
- ❏ Screwdriver
- ❏ Lubricant(s)
- ❏ Small cup

The alcohol must be "technical grade," which means that it must be of at least 96 percent purity, and preferably higher. It should not be used on plastic or rubber parts. For this you will need a cleaning solvent meant for this task (i.e., be sure that the label says that the solvent leaves no residues and is safe for plastic and rubber parts). This solvent can be used for all cleaning; however, it is more expensive than the alcohol.

The lubricant should be of the nonpetroleum variety, and must be nonconductive. Oil is used in most places; grease is needed for gears. These are available in some electronics supply stores, camera shops and even building material stores. Do not use spray lubricants.

MAINTENANCE SCHEDULE

The following table is a general maintenance schedule. It is based on average conditions and average player use. If your conditions are worse, or your use of the player is more frequent, you will probably have to perform the steps more often than shown. Some of the steps, such as cleaning the discs and checking the conditions, can be done on an "as needed" basis.

Months	3	6	9	12
Clean exterior	*	*	*	*
Clean discs		*		*
Clean lens	*	*	*	*
Clean interior		*		*
Check remote battery		*		*
Lubricate rails			*	
Lubricate slide			*	
Check cables and connectors				*

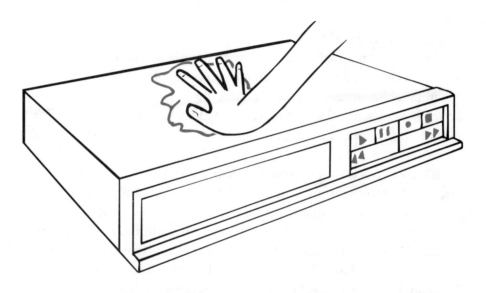

Step 5-1. Cleaning the cabinet and disc tray.
Clean the cabinet with a cloth. This keeps the unit looking more attractive. More important, it reduces the amount of dust that seeps inside. The disc tray can be cleaned with a lint-free cloth. A swab slightly dampened with cleaner can be used to clean the corners. If possible, keep the player covered when not in use, but remove the cover when you are using the machine.

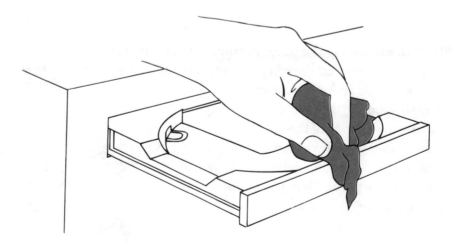

Step 5-2. Getting inside.

The instruction manuals that come with CD players do not tell you how to get inside. Yet, this is necessary to complete the cleaning and general maintenance. (*Caution:* Opening the cabinet while the player is under warranty could void that warranty.) Fortunately, getting inside is easy. With most CD players, the top cover is held in place by two or four screws.

If only two screws are used, they will be at the back and either through the top or through the sides. There also might be screws in the back. Examine your unit and find the holding screws. Shut off the power and unplug the unit. Remove the screws carefully and put them in a small cup. Lift the cover at the rear while gently pulling backwards to release the lip that holds the cover at the front. If the cover doesn't lift easily, carefully inspect the player for screws you've missed.

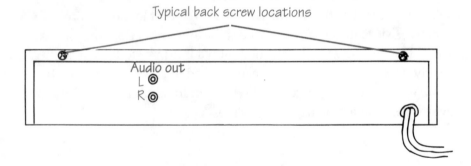

Typical back screw locations

Audio out
L
R

Step 5-3. Examining the inner components of the player.

Once you've removed the top cover you can get at the various circuits and mechanisms. Before beginning, thoroughly examine the interior of the player to identify the various parts and pieces, and to determine how you can safely get at them. Clean the general interior.

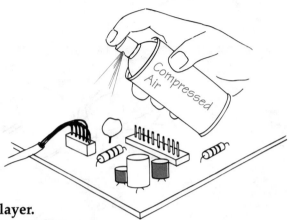

Step 5-4. Cleaning the interior of the player.
To clean the general interior, use a lint-free cloth slightly
dampened with cleaning fluid or alcohol. A swab
dampened with cleaning fluid or alcohol can be used
to get into the corners and other tight spots. Also a
can of dry compressed air, such as that purchased in
camera stores, is good for cleaning dust from difficult
to reach areas.

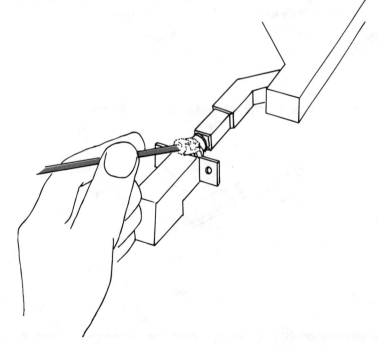

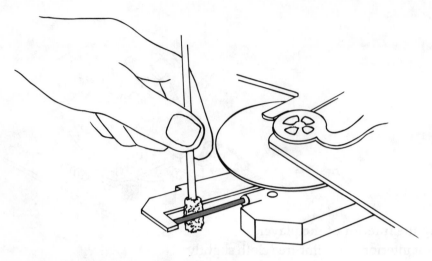

Step 5-5. Cleaning the RAIL assembly.

Locate the laser assembly. If it is of the type that uses rails (the most common), dampen a swab with the cleaning fluid and gently "wash" the rails behind the assembly. Be sure to clean all the way around both rails, and not just the tops. Most of the time there will also be a very small part of the rails ahead of the assembly. You might need to use a flashlight to locate this because of the tight quarters. Keep in mind that these spots are parts of the same rails. Once you have found them, carefully clean both sides with a dampened swab.

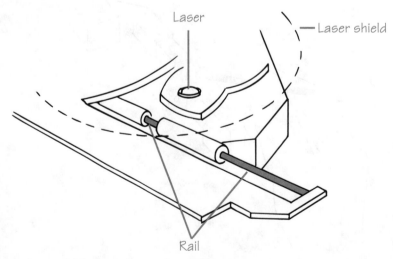

Front portion of rail is located under laser shield across from laser.

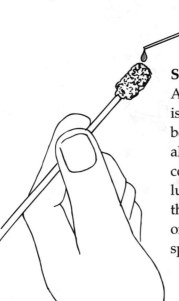

Step 5-6. Lubricating the rails.

Apply a small amount of lubricant to the rails. This is essential whenever the rails have been cleaned because the cleaning process removes lubricant along with the contaminants. To have maximum control, it's usually best to place a small drop of lubricant on a swab and then use the swab to spread this on the rails. Be very careful to put the lubricant only on the rails and nowhere else. Do not use a spray lubricant!

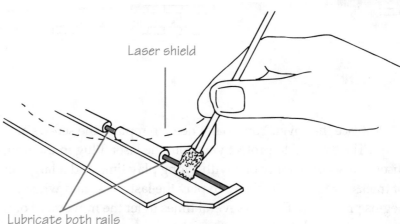

Laser shield

Lubricate both rails

Step 5-7. Cleaning a swing arm type assembly.

If your player uses a swing arm type assembly, the
cleaning procedure is much the same. Carefully clean the
arm with a dampened swab. Then apply a small and
controlled amount of lubricant to the pin on which
the arm rotates and/or to the arm itself if it slides
through a stabilizing device.

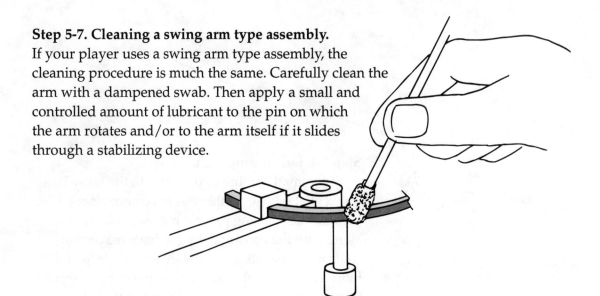

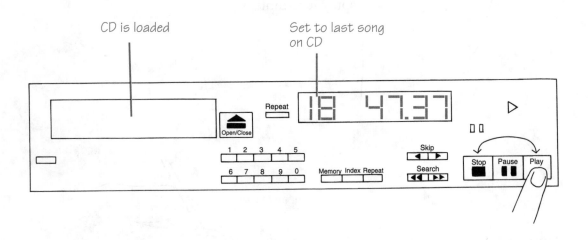

CD is loaded

Set to last song
on CD

Replace the cover. You do not need to replace the screws at this
point. The cover is to protect you from the laser. Plug in the unit, then
insert a disc, preferably one with a long play time and a large number
of tracks. Program the player to play the last track, and when the play
begins press Stop. Do this several times to let the movement of the
assembly spread the lubricant evenly.

Step 5-8. Correcting a jamming disc drawer.
If the disc drawer is binding, examine all parts that cause its movement. These vary from machine to machine. In general, the drawer will slide along bars on each side. If binding is a problem, clean and lubricate these bars. Run the drawer in and out several times to evenly spread the lubricant. (*Note*: this step and the next are not a part of regular maintenance but are steps that should be taken only when necessary.)

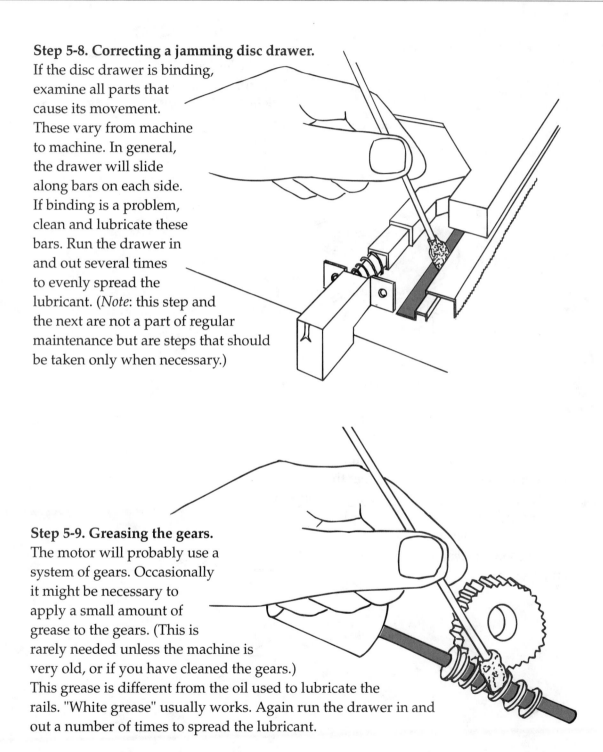

Step 5-9. Greasing the gears.
The motor will probably use a system of gears. Occasionally it might be necessary to apply a small amount of grease to the gears. (This is rarely needed unless the machine is very old, or if you have cleaned the gears.)
This grease is different from the oil used to lubricate the rails. "White grease" usually works. Again run the drawer in and out a number of times to spread the lubricant.

Step 5-10. Cleaning the lenses.

Contaminants can block the laser beam(s). Locate the lens and clean it carefully with the cleaning fluid and a swab. It is critical that you use a cleaner safe for this lens and that will not leave a residue or cause *fogging*. The lens in less expensive units might be made of plastic.

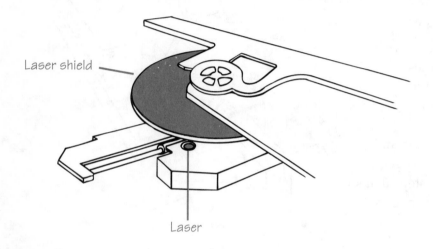

Step 5-11. Cleaning cable connectors.

Sometimes the only problem is that the cable connectors need to be cleaned. Larger connectors, such as those that connect the CD player to the stereo, can be cleaned with alcohol or cleaning fluid and a swab.

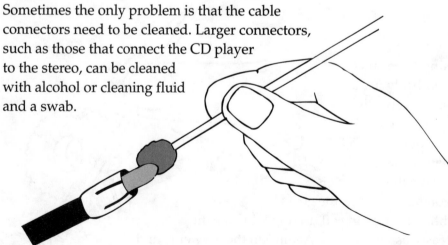

Step 5-12.

Spray cleaning circuit board connectors.
Some connectors, such as those for circuit
boards, have delicate pins. It's best to use a
spray cleaner for these so that the pins
don't get bent or damaged. It's
relatively rare that these need
cleaning. Do so only when
necessary, such as if there is visible
corrosion or discoloring of the pins. (*Caution:*
Do not use a spray cleaner with any kind of
lubricant or residue of any kind in it. Read the
label carefully.)

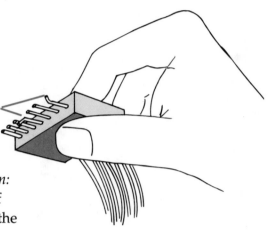

Bent pins

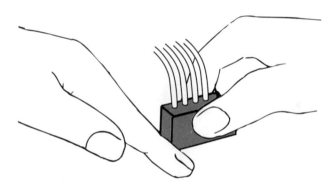

To remove a circuit board
connector, first inspect it for any
catches, holding screws, etc. Grasp
it between your finger and thumb.
Hold the circuit board with your
other hand. (This is to prevent it
from moving.) Pull gently. Do not
force it!

To spray clean the
connector, spray away
from yourself. Use the
spray sparingly.

CHAPTER SIX

The Discs

When CDs first appeared on the market, salesmen were fond of claiming that compact discs could be scratched, marred, contaminated, and otherwise abused with no effect on the playback quality. One early advertisement had a person smearing peanut butter on the disc to show how it would still play. What most people didn't notice was that the peanut butter was placed on the label side rather than on the clear side. The advertisement also didn't show what was undoubtedly a very messy (possibly terminally so) CD player afterwards.

It's true that compact discs are not nearly as prone to wear or damage as records are; however, they are not immune to damage. They must be cared for in order to last. If the player is playing poorly, the problem is more likely to be with the disc than with the machine. Take care of your discs to avoid a lot of trouble.

Step 6-1. Storing the discs.

When not in use, always keep the discs stored in their containers and ideally in a cabinet or CD holder.

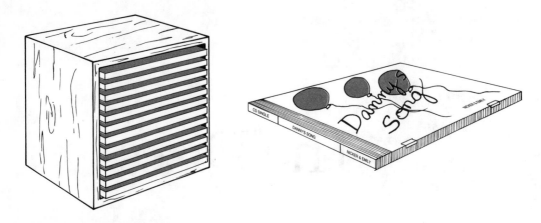

Step 6-2. Handling the discs.

When removing a CD from the container, it is best to grasp the edges with two fingers while another finger presses against the tines that hold the disc. Handle the discs by the edges only.

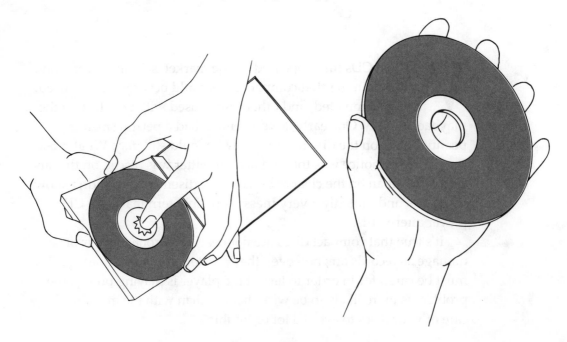

Step 6-3. Keeping CDs from hazardous conditions.

Compact discs are sensitive to heat, which can cause the plastic to warp or even melt. Keep them away from all sources of heat. This caution can be particularly important when CDs are kept in a car. Protecting the player from adverse conditions is important. As with the disc itself, the player must be kept away from sources of heat and sunlight. Cigarette smoke is a major cause of internal gumming and other problems.

Warp

Step 6-4. Loading the disc into the player.

Insert the disc carefully into the player. Make sure that it is flat and centered in the tray. Not doing so won't damage the disc or the machine, but the unit won't be able to play the disc.

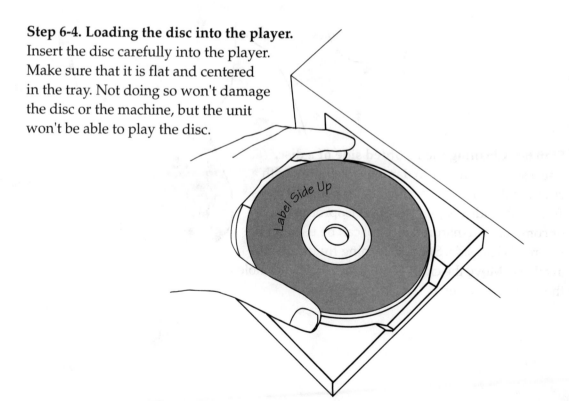

Label Side Up

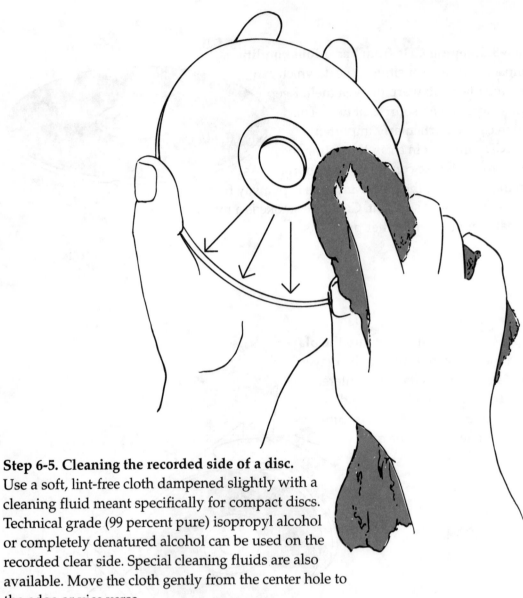

Step 6-5. Cleaning the recorded side of a disc.
Use a soft, lint-free cloth dampened slightly with a
cleaning fluid meant specifically for compact discs.
Technical grade (99 percent pure) isopropyl alcohol
or completely denatured alcohol can be used on the
recorded clear side. Special cleaning fluids are also
available. Move the cloth gently from the center hole to
the edge or vice versa.

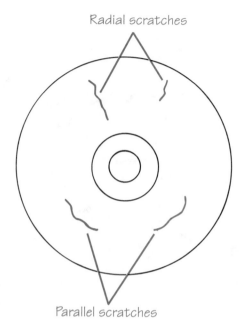

Radial scratches

Parallel scratches

Step 6-6. Avoiding scratches.

Do not wipe the disc in a circular motion. This increases the chances of causing radial scratches, which are much more prone to causing irregular playback. Do not scrub.

Scratches can be one of two types: radial (around) and perpendicular (across). Perpendicular scratches might remove recorded bits on a number of tracks, but many players will be able to ignore small scratches.

Radial scratches, dust, and grime might remove or cover more recorded bits on the same track, thus interrupting the laser beam. This can cause severe skipping, and is why cleaning the disc should be done from center to edge, or edge to center, rather than around the disc.

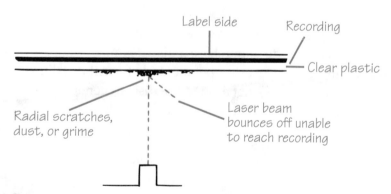

Label side

Recording

Clear plastic

Radial scratches, dust, or grime

Laser beam bounces off unable to reach recording

Step 6-7. Cleaning with air.
If the disc is especially dirty with visible particles, blow it off, preferably with dry compressed air, before inserting it into your machine. This will help prevent scratches.

Step 6-8. Cleaning with a specialty product.
If you decide to purchase a disc cleaning unit, be sure that it cleans perpendicularly (it will usually say so on the box), not around the disc. In general, you can do a better and safer cleaning job by hand.

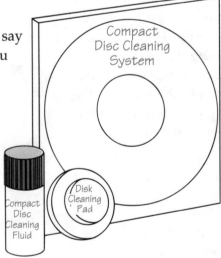

Step 6-9. Cleaning the label side of discs.
Because many labels are printed with alcohol-based inks, using alcohol
on the label side can erase or smear the label. Some cleaning fluids,
such as those meant for records, can cause other damage like fogging.

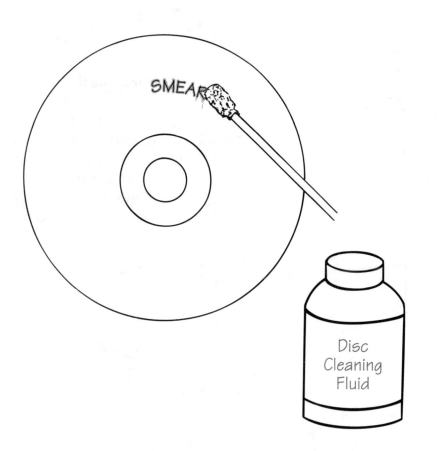

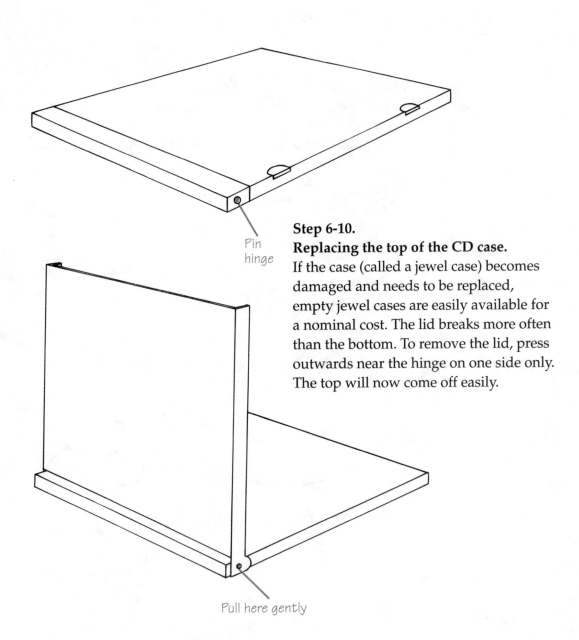

Pin
hinge

Pull here gently

Step 6-10.
Replacing the top of the CD case.
If the case (called a jewel case) becomes
damaged and needs to be replaced,
empty jewel cases are easily available for
a nominal cost. The lid breaks more often
than the bottom. To remove the lid, press
outwards near the hinge on one side only.
The top will now come off easily.

Step 6-11. Swapping labels.
Remove the surface label from the
damaged lid and place it in the new lid.

Step 6-12. Replacing the bottom case.
If the case needs to be replaced, lift the CD holder from the
bottom of the case from the hinged side of the case.

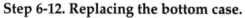

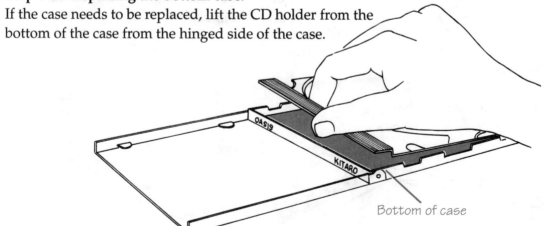

Bottom of case

Remove the lower label.

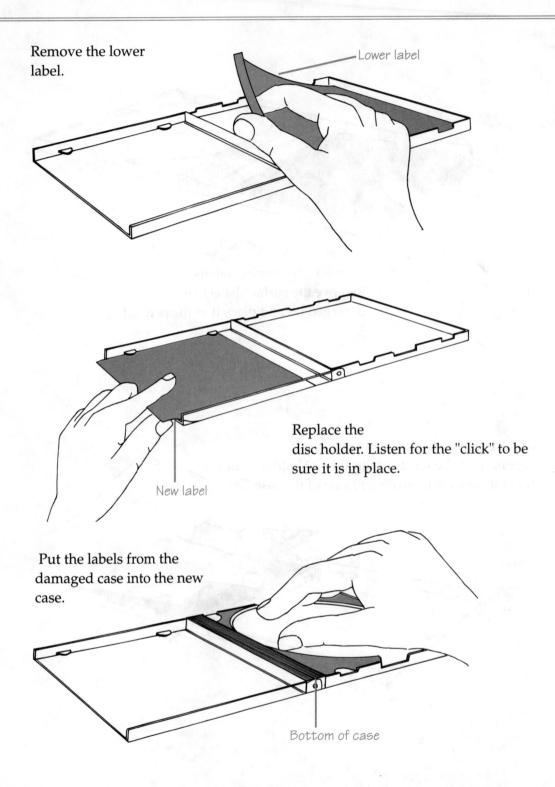

Lower label

New label

Replace the disc holder. Listen for the "click" to be sure it is in place.

Put the labels from the damaged case into the new case.

Bottom of case

CHAPTER SEVEN

Problem Areas and Operations

Each CD player make and model is different. There are even greater differences when you consider the system as a whole. Your unit might not be like the illustrations. Because of this, it's important for you to compare your own player and system with the machines used for these illustrations. You'll find differences, but you'll also find many similarities.

Much of it is common sense. Remember, things work in a certain way for a certain reason—and when they fail, there is a reason for that as well. For example, if a cable or wire comes loose, it won't be able to carry the signals to the next component. The same is true of other problems. A part might be obviously broken or bent. Even the components and circuit boards sometimes reveal the cause of the problem by simply looking.

The first step in solving a problem is determining the symptoms—what is happening, or not happening? If you think it will help, write a list of the symptoms along with your best guesses as to what might be causing the problem. This will help you to eliminate where the problem is not.

Step 7-1. Checking each unit that makes up your system.
Unless you already know that the problem is definitely in a particular
component (e.g., in the player), don't forget that the problem could be
caused by any of the pieces. Jot down the symptoms you've noticed.
Then check the obvious first. Is the stereo on? Is it set to play from the
CD player? Are the speakers connected? It sometimes helps to draw a
block diagram of that system, with the boxes representing the various
pieces of the system. Visually examine each piece in the system to be
sure that each is properly connected.

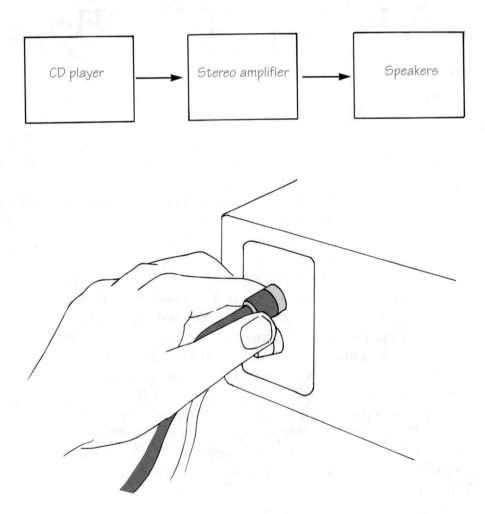

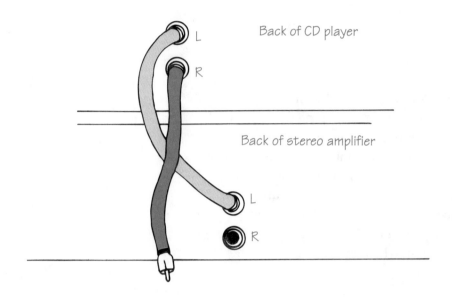

Step 7-2. Removing
the cabinet and looking inside.

Remove the cabinet as instructed in Step 5-2. Visually examine the
internal components of the unit.
In this exaggerated example,
notice that a wire on one of
the connectors is broken,
that a capacitor on a
circuit board has
broken open
and burned, and that
somehow a paper clip
got inside and is causing a short.

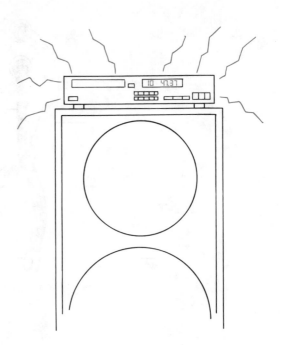

Step 7-3. Avoiding vibration.

Problems such as skipping can be caused by something as simple as improper placement of the unit. CD players are just as sensitive to vibration as are record turntables, and in some ways are even more sensitive. Placing the unit on a loudspeaker could be causing excessive vibration, which in turn can make the unit skip.

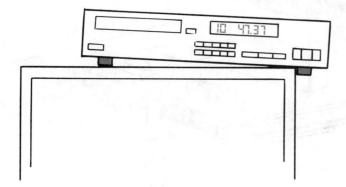

The vibration-absorbing feet on the bottom of the unit might be worn or missing. This is rare, but possible nonetheless. Also, if the unit isn't located on a flat surface, with all four feet on that surface, they can't absorb vibration.

Step 7-4. Providing adequate ventilation.

The circuits in the player generate some heat while operating. Most CD players vent this by convection through holes in the cabinet. If the holes are blocked, either top or bottom, heat can build up inside and cause damage. Be sure that the player's vent holes are open and unblocked. Do not set it on a surface such as a rug or a bed.

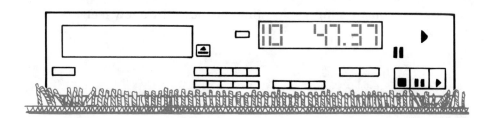

Step 7-5. Avoiding hazardous elements.

Do not place your player in direct sunlight, excessive heat, and certainly areas that are dirty. (This includes cigarette smoke, which can "gum up" both the discs and the player quickly.)

Step 7-6. Transporting the player properly.
Many units have a locking screw or screws located possibly in the back
but usually beneath the unit. These are meant to hold the laser
assembly still when the unit is moved from place to place. After
purchasing a new player, you must remove these screws. Keep these
screws around; you can tape them inside the owner's manual so you
don't lose them. Be sure to remove any disc that might be in the player
and then replace the screws before transporting the player. This is not
necessary if you are simply relocating the player by a few feet.

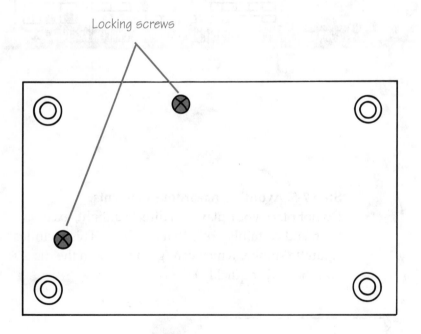

Locking screws

Step 7-7. Checking cables.

Often a cable will appear to be just fine when in fact it has a problem inside. The easiest and fastest way to test is to try using a different cable you know to be good. Remove the suspected cable and replace it with another. If the system works, you have found the problem.

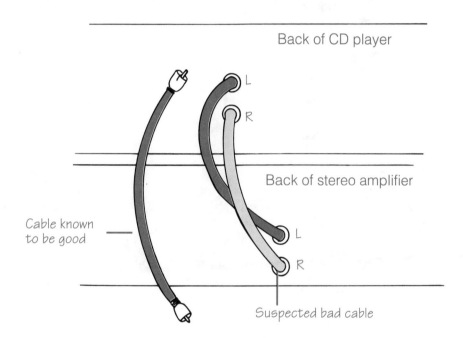

Back of CD player

L

R

Back of stereo amplifier

Cable known
to be good

L

R

Suspected bad cable

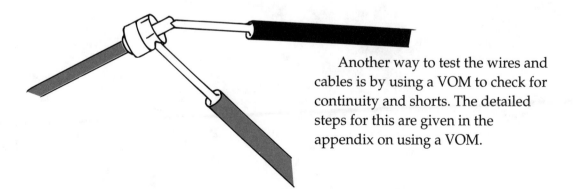

Another way to test the wires and cables is by using a VOM to check for continuity and shorts. The detailed steps for this are given in the appendix on using a VOM.

CHAPTER EIGHT

Connections

A CD player by itself is useless. To play back it must be connected to a stereo system, which must in turn be connected to speakers. (Some players have a built-in amplifier to drive a set of headphones, without the need of a separate stereo amplifier, but the principle is the same.)

Most people simply connect the player to the stereo, then the stereo to the speakers. Often this is done using nothing more than the cables and wires that came with the various units, or something similar.

When you buy a new CD player, the basic cables come with it. These are adequate for a standard hookup. Additional wires, cables, connectors, and so forth can be purchased. These can expand your versatility. This chapter explains which wire, cables, and connectors you need, and for what purposes.

Step 8-1. Connecting the CD player to the stereo.
The standard connection between the CD player and the stereo uses two cables, each with RCA-type connectors. One cable is for the left channel and one for the right channel. The output connectors on the CD player connect to the appropriate input connectors on the stereo amplifier. These cables are usually no more than 2 or 3 feet in length, which is generally sufficient because the player is usually located close to the stereo amplifier. Longer cables are available. If you wish, you can build your own cables, customized to the needed length.

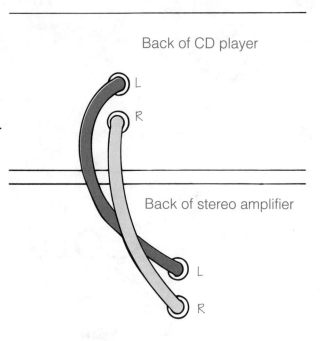

Back of CD player

Back of stereo amplifier

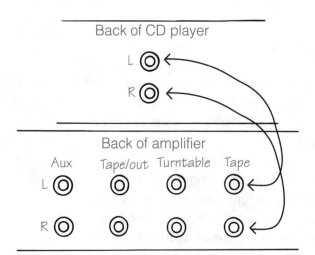

Step 8-2. Checking the impedance.
In many cases the stereo amplifier will have specific CD player inputs. In older stereo units, there might be no such input. Instead you might find one labeled AUX (auxiliary), or perhaps one that says LINE INPUT. The CD player will function with these. The switching knob for these inputs is on the stereo's control panel.

Step 8-3. Using other connections.

Lacking this option, most inputs to the stereo amplifier will work. For example, if you have a CD player but no turntable, and the stereo has a turntable input, chances are you can connect your CD player there. The stereo also might have some input you are not using, such as TAPE. Take advantage of any unused inputs.

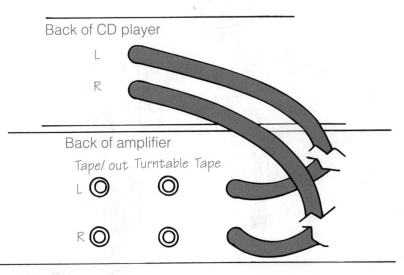

Step 8-4. Connecting stereo outputs.

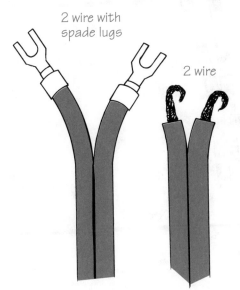

Speakers can be connected to the stereo in any of several ways. One is to use the same kind of RCA-typed connectors that hook the CD player to the stereo. Another is to use 2-wire cord. This might end as either bare wire (twisted together and preferably tinned with solder) or it might have spade lugs.

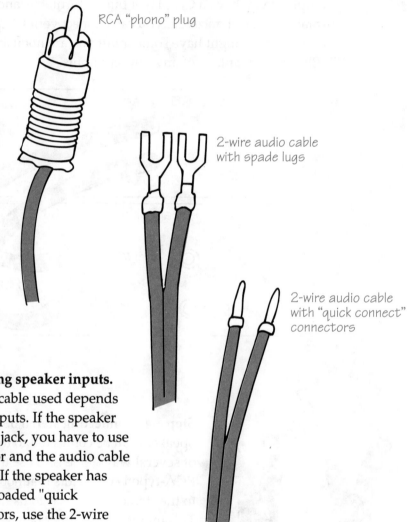

RCA "phono" plug

2-wire audio cable with spade lugs

2-wire audio cable with "quick connect" connectors

Step 8-5. Checking speaker inputs.
The type of wire cable used depends on the speaker inputs. If the speaker has only an RCA jack, you have to use an RCA connector and the audio cable that goes with it. If the speaker has screw or spring-loaded "quick connect" connectors, use the 2-wire cord.

Step 8-6. Extending the speaker system.

With the superior audio quality available with CDs, you might be inclined to move your speakers farther apart to get a stronger stereo separation. Or you might wish to locate a pair of speakers elsewhere in the home. This means using a length of the needed cable or cord. Because you can't buy the specific length premade, you have to make your own. Fortunately this is easy to do.

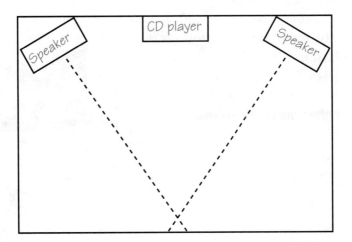

Step 8-7. Running a 2-wire speaker cord.

This kind of cord is similar to standard electrical zip cord. You can use this kind of electrical cord for speakers; however, the zip cord is not purposely designed for low resistance and the wires are not marked for polarity. This cord consists of two wire sets, each separately insulated. The wire itself is stranded. Except for special circumstances, solid wire is not suitable for speaker installations.

Two-wire cord can be purchased in almost any length and in several sizes. In general, the longer the run, the larger the wire should be. For most installations, 16 gauge will do fine; 14 gauge is slightly larger and is used for longer runs. It is not usually advisable to use wire smaller than 20 gauge, nor is it necessary to use wire larger than 12 gauge. Spools of 25, 50, and 100 feet are readily available. Many stores carry larger spools from which you can purchase any length you wish. Don't try to measure too accurately; it is better to have a few extra feet than to have the wire come up short.

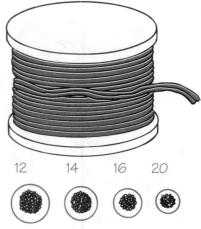

12   14   16   20

Enlarged to show detail

2–3″

Step 8-8. Preparing the wire.
Once you have the cord, pull the two
wires apart. You need about two or three
inches of separated cord.

Step 8-9. Stripping the wires.
The best way to strip the insulation
from the wire is to use the wire
stripper described in chapter 2.
 If you use a knife, be extremely
careful to avoid cutting into the
wire. Strip about 1/2 inch of the
insulation from the wire.

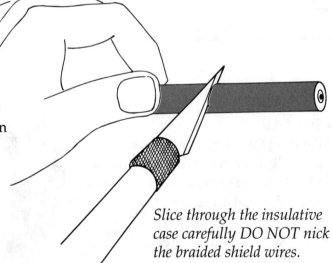

*Slice through the insulative
case carefully DO NOT nick
the braided shield wires.*

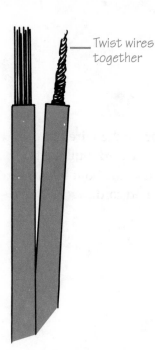

Twist wires together

Step 8-10.
Twisting the wires together.
Twist the wires together and then make sure there are no loose strands. These can cause short circuits between the speaker terminals. If you have the ability, it is best to *tin* the ends with solder.

Step 8-11.
Bending the wires into a hook.
Carefully bend the end of the wires into a hook. A pair of needle-nose pliers can be used to make a smooth hook.

Step 8-12. Connecting the hook to the screw terminal. Check again to be sure there are no loose strands. Place the hook beneath the screw terminal so that the hook is in the same direction that the screw tightens (clockwise).

Before tightening the screw, use the blade of the screwdriver to tuck the hook completely beneath the screw head so it is wrapped partially around the screw shaft. Tighten the screw, then check again for loose strands.

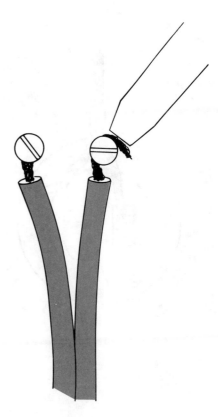

Step 8-13. Installing a spade lug.

A more secure installation is possible by using a U-shaped spade lug. Be sure to choose one meant from the screw terminal size of the speaker. The lug fits beneath the screw head and around the shaft. Some lugs require solder and some come in the solderless variety. In the latter case, the terminal is crimped into place with a crimper or a pair of pliers.

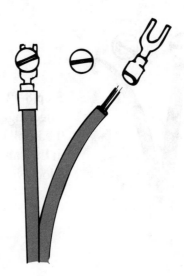

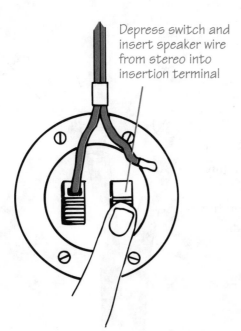

Depress switch and insert speaker wire from stereo into insertion terminal

Step 8-14. Using quick-connect speaker connectors.

Some speakers, especially the more expensive ones, have spring-loaded quick connect buttons. Pushing the button opens a slot through which the wire can be placed. When the button is released, a slide closes on the wire and makes a firm connection. As with using the screw terminal, it is best that the wire be tinned with solder.

Step 8-15. Using audio cable for speaker connections.
If the speaker has only an RCA-type jack, you have to use audio cable and RCA plugs. This cable has a center conductor of stranded wire, a layer of insulation, a braided shield, and an outer layer of insulation. Although a special wire stripper is available to prepare the cable, some prefer to do the job with a knife. If you use a knife, be careful not to nick the conductors. First cut away about 1/2 inch of the outer insulation, being careful to avoid the braided shield beneath. Next, use a point to separate the braids. Pull these to one side and twist them tightly together. Check to be sure there are no loose strands.

Cut away 1/4 to 3/4 inch of the insulation around the center conductor. Be careful not to cut into or damage the braided shield beneath.

Use a point to separate the braids.

Pull the braids to one side and twist them together tightly. Check to be sure that there are on loose strands.

Twist the center strands tightly and check for loose strands.

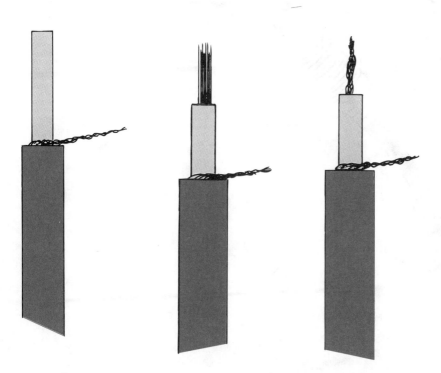

Step 8-16. Differentiating between solder and solderless plugs.
Unless you can solder, you must specify that the RCA (phono) plug is
of the solderless type. The plug on the left has a hole in the center shaft.
This requires solder. The plug on the right has a screw for the center
conductor and wings that clamp on the braid. This kind of connector is
less secure, but no soldering is needed. In either case, be sure to put the
outer shell of the connector plug over the wire before installing the
plug itself.

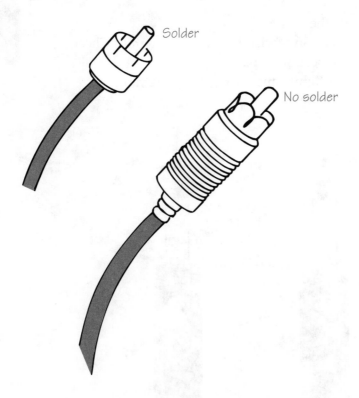

Step 8-17. Installing RCA plugs.

Strip the cable as in step 8-9. Wrap the center conductor around the screw in a clockwise direction and tuck it beneath the screw head. Tighten this screw and check for loose strands. Place the twisted braid in the wings and crimp them shut. Place the plug cover over the completed connector.

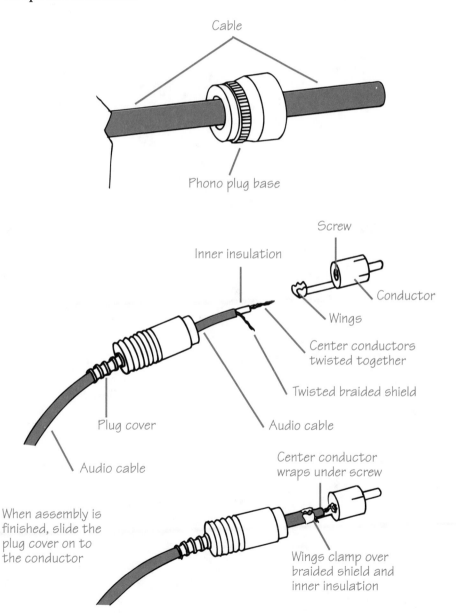

Cable

Phono plug base

Screw

Inner insulation

Conductor

Wings

Center conductors twisted together

Twisted braided shield

Plug cover

Audio cable

Audio cable

Center conductor wraps under screw

When assembly is finished, slide the plug cover on to the conductor

Wings clamp over braided shield and inner insulation

CHAPTER NINE

Portable Players

Portable units differ from the home models in a number of ways. Obviously they are smaller and lighter. Many of the portable units aren't much larger than the CD itself. The home unit plugs into an outlet, whereas the portable player requires batteries or an ac/dc adapter and the automobile player uses power generated from the car's electrical system. The home unit is meant to send its signals to the home stereo where it is amplified and sent to the speakers. The portable unit might have this same function, it might have its own amplifier (such as with a car unit), or it might be meant to drive earphones only.

In general, the troubleshooting and maintenance processes are similar to that of larger home-type CD players. The major difference is how you get at the various parts. Sometimes (such as cleaning the laser lens) this is very easy. Other times (cleaning or lubricating the rails) it requires some fairly extensive disassembly.

Step 9-1. Examining your player.

Before you begin any troubleshooting, repair, or even maintenance you need to be familiar with the unit and its features. How does it open? Where are the controls? Does the unit use batteries or does it get its power through an adapter jack? What safety features are present? How is the player connected to the speakers or headphones?

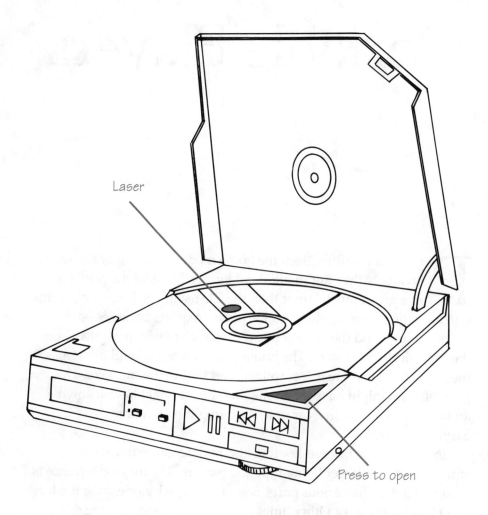

Laser

Press to open

Step 9-2. Becoming familiar with the controls.

The main controls are always on the front panel and are similar to those of the home unit. The power switch might be obvious, or it might be tucked away where it is less visible.

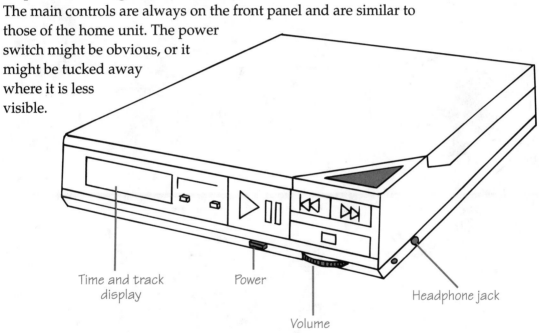

Time and track display

Power

Volume

Headphone jack

Step 9-3. Testing the incoming power from an adapter.
If the unit is completely dead, it could be that the incoming power isn't
getting to the machine. The adapter can be tested easily with a VOM.
Set the VOM to read dc voltage in the proper range. With portable CD
players that use an adapter, this is almost always 9 volts. Probe the
connector as shown. If the adapter has no voltage output, the unit isn't
being powered. Replace the adapter.

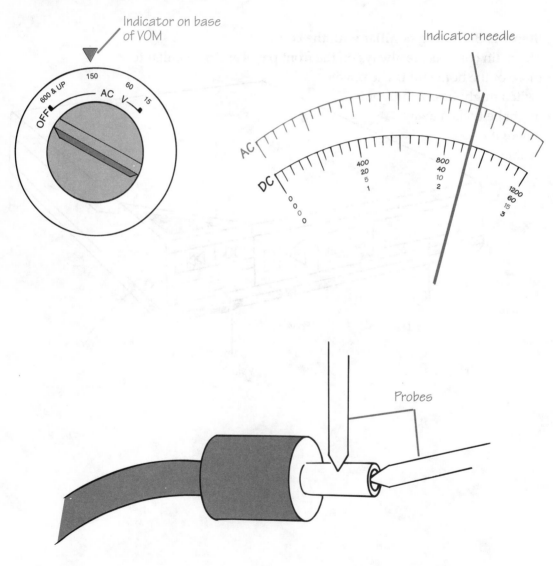

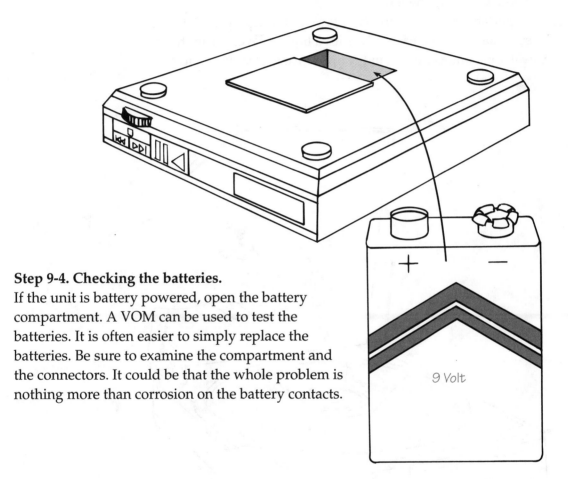

Step 9-4. Checking the batteries.
If the unit is battery powered, open the battery
compartment. A VOM can be used to test the
batteries. It is often easier to simply replace the
batteries. Be sure to examine the compartment and
the connectors. It could be that the whole problem is
nothing more than corrosion on the battery contacts.

Step 9-5. Cleaning the lens.

Most portable units are top loading. With the top opened, the laser can be seen and accessed easily. As with a home player, clean the lens with a swab or chamois dipped in the appropriate cleaning fluid.

Step 9-6. Opening the case.

The screws that hold the case together are small. You need a fine jeweler's screwdriver with a phillips-type head. Because the screws are so small, before attempting to remove them, set the player on a flat surface so that the screws don't fall off and get lost.

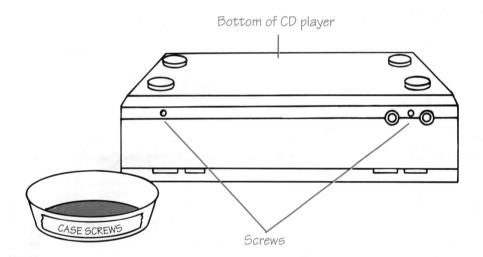

Bottom of CD player

CASE SCREWS

Screws

Step 9-7. Examining the interior.
Examine the interior carefully before proceeding. Often there are fine wires and thin connectors that go from the circuit board to the other parts of the player. All of these are extremely delicate and are easily damaged. Use a lint-free cloth to clean the parts you can get to. See step 5-4. Depending on the design, you might not be able do any more without desoldering at least one connector. In most cases, you cannot get at the rails or other interior mechanisms without removing the circuit board.

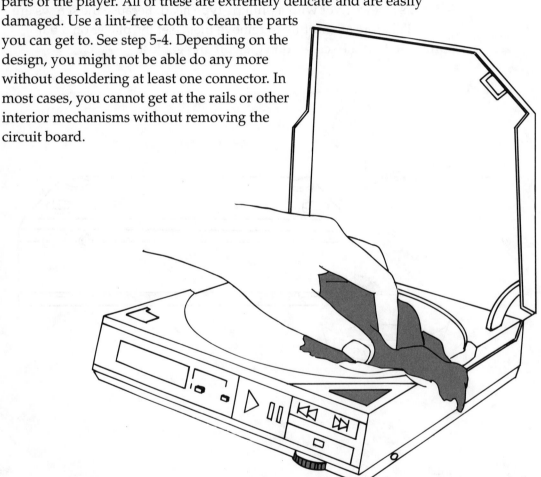

Step 9-8. Detaching the circuit board.

After you have examined the interior and have determined that you can safely proceed, look over the circuit board for the holding screws.

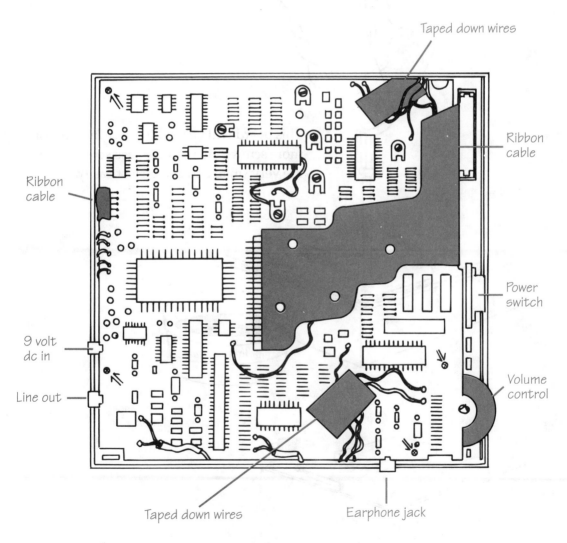

Typical circuit board.

This board will be held in place by three or more screws. As with the case screws, these are very small and can be lost easily.

Holding screws

Note the difference between the screws

Adjustment screw

Holding screw

Before lifting the circuit board, study the delicate wires and other connectors. If there is any resistance, examine the board more carefully. Do not force it in any way.

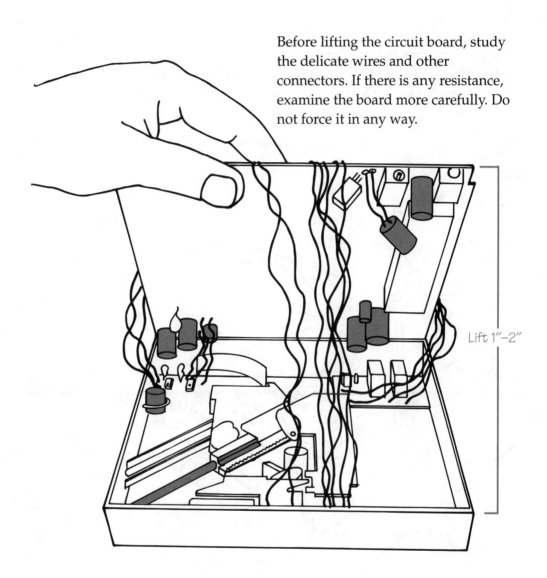

Lift 1″–2″

Step 9-9. Servicing the interior.

With the circuit board out of the way, you have access to the interior. The rails can be cleaned and lubricated as in steps 5-5 and 5-6.

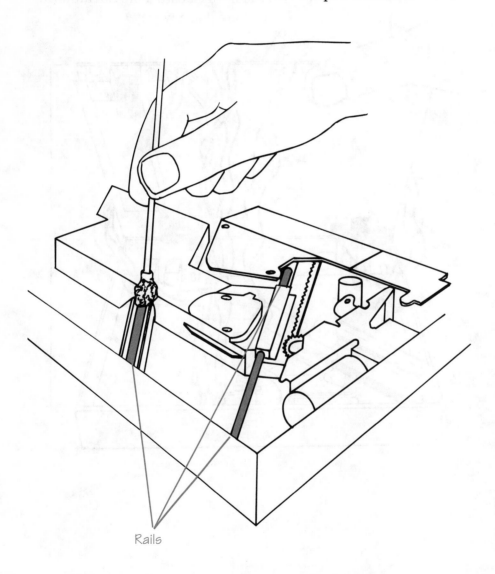

Rails

Step 9-10. Caring for portables.

Because the unit is portable, it is easy to forget that it can be affected by all of the same things that damage the home unit. The portable CD player is meant to be fairly tough, but one look inside reveals that it is very delicate. Keep it out of sunlight, away from excessive heat and moisture, and try to minimize vibrations. The general rule of thumb is that if the conditions are uncomfortable for you, the CD player should not be there, nor should the CDs. Keep your CDs in a case when you transport them.

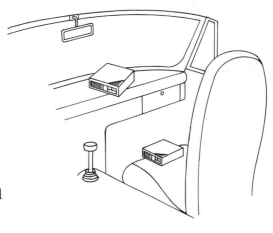

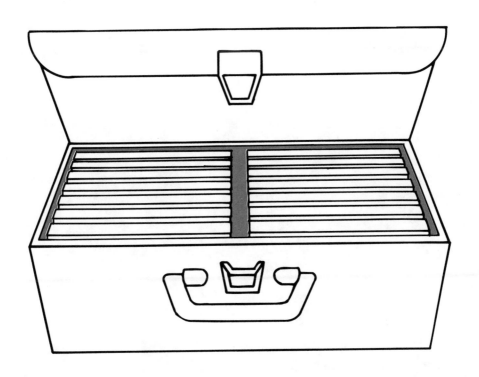

How to Use a VOM

Some of the tests in this book require a volt-ohmmeter (VOM, also called a multimeter). A VOM is a handy and versatile piece of testing equipment, and it's easy to use.

With a VOM, you can test any batteries you use—including the one in your car. You also can test the wall outlets to see if they have power and if they have been wired correctly (and to make sure they are safe). You can test wires, cables, and connectors to see if they need to be replaced.

The VOM you buy doesn't have to be fancy or expensive. A model costing between $10 and $20 should suffice. Extreme accuracy isn't usually needed. When checking a wall outlet for power, you rarely need accuracy of greater than about 10 percent. Even the least expensive units are more accurate than that.

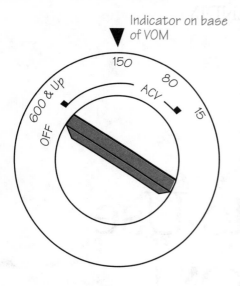

Indicator on base of VOM

A VOM tests for ac voltage, dc voltage, and resistance. A number of ranges are available on the VOM for each test. The most common ac test checks the wall outlets in your home; your meter should have a setting for the 120-volt ac range. Common dc tests involve in or near typical battery outputs—namely 1.5, 3, 5-6, 9, and 12. Make sure your voltage setting is higher than the voltage you are testing, so you don't damage the VOM. For example, if you are expecting to read 120-volts ac, you would set the meter to the 150 setting. If you are uncertain of the value, start at the highest setting and work downwards.

Step A-1. Setting up the meter.

For almost every test, plug the shorter end of the black lead into the "common" (–) jack on the meter. The shorter end of the red lead gets plugged into the + jack, which is often labeled as shown.

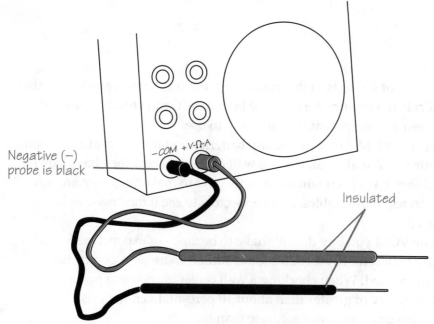

Negative (–) probe is black

Insulated

Step A-2. Setting the Ohms Adjust to zero.

To set the "Ohms Adjust," turn on the meter, set the dial to read resistance (any range), touch the two probes together, and turn the adjusting wheel until the reading is exactly zero.

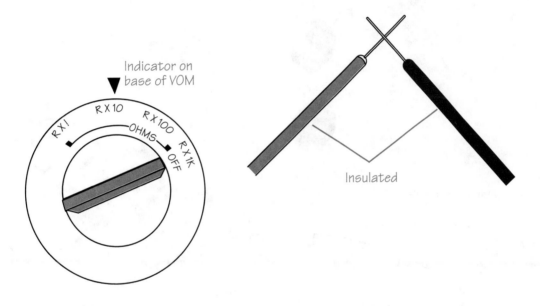

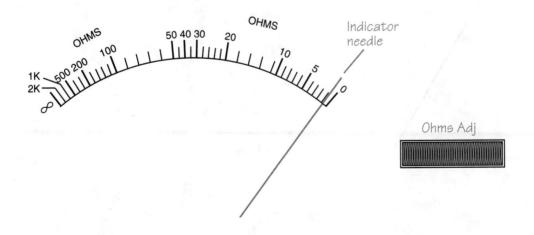

Step A-3. Setting the Zero Adjust.

If your meter has a "Zero Adjust," turn on the meter and adjust the control knob so that the meter reads exactly zero.

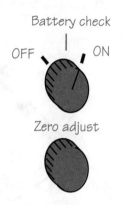

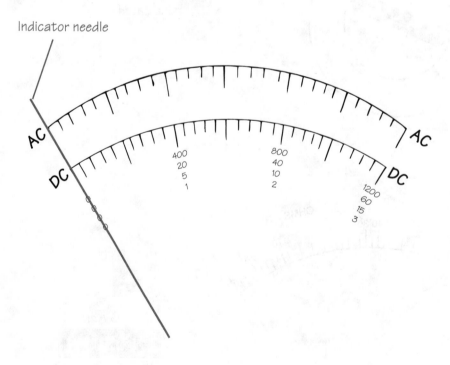

Step A-4. Reading dc volts.

To read dc volts (dc V or sometimes Vdc), set the meter to the proper range. Touch the black probe to the side with the negative (– or GND) label, and touch the red probe to the side with the positive (+) label.

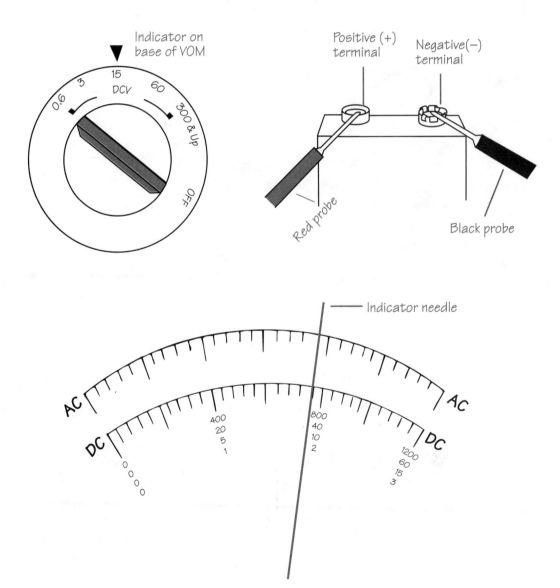

Step A-5. Testing a battery.

To test a battery, the positive terminal is usually round and is often labeled. Set the meter to read dc in the appropriate range. (AAA, AA, C, and D are all 1.5 volts. On most other batteries, the voltage is clearly labeled.)

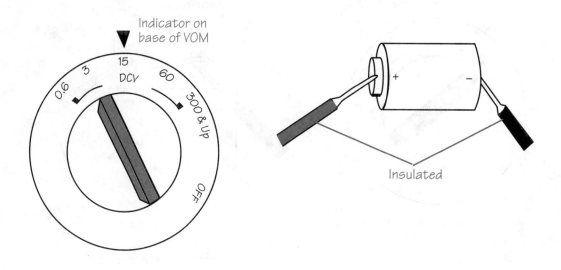

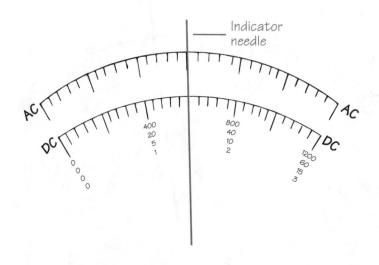

Step A-6. Testing for ac voltage.
When testing for ac voltage, the orientation of the probes is not important because the ac voltage is constantly changing from negative to positive and from positive to negative. Because ac is generally much more dangerous to you, it is essential that you hold the probes only by the insulated handles.

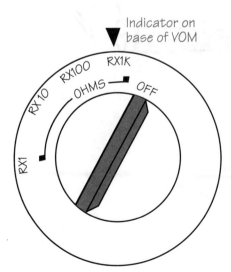

Indicator on
base of VOM

Step A-7. Testing for continuity.
In this book, the most important resistance (ohms) test is for continuity, which simply means that the conductor being tested is continuous (not broken). Although the setting used is not important, it's best to use the highest setting (for resistance or ohms) on the dial.

Conductor

Step A-8. Checking for continuity.

Disconnect the wire or cable that is to be tested. Touch the probes to each end of the same conductor. It doesn't matter which probe touches which end. If the conductor is good, the needle should swing all the way to the right, giving a reading of zero ohms (or close to it). If there is a break in the wire, the reading will be close to infinity (full left scale and no needle movement).

Step A-9. Testing for a short.

To test for a short in a cable, touch one probe to the center conductor and the other to the outer ground. (Repeat this test using the center conductor at one end and the outer ground at the other.) If the cable is good, the reading should be infinity (full left scale and no needle movement). If the meter gives any reading (any needle movement), the two conductors are touching.
If the meter swings all the way to zero ohms, the conductors are in direct contact, which is a short circuit; the cable is bad.

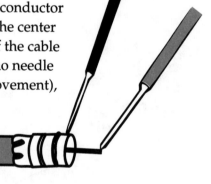

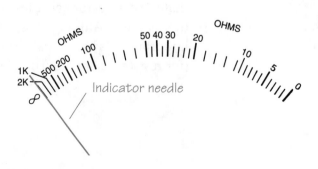

Indicator needle

Step A-10.
Testing for dc on a circuit board.
When testing for dc on a circuit board, look
for the label or GND. Touch the black probe
to it and the red probe to the other dc point
being tested. This will often be labeled
something like +5 or +12.

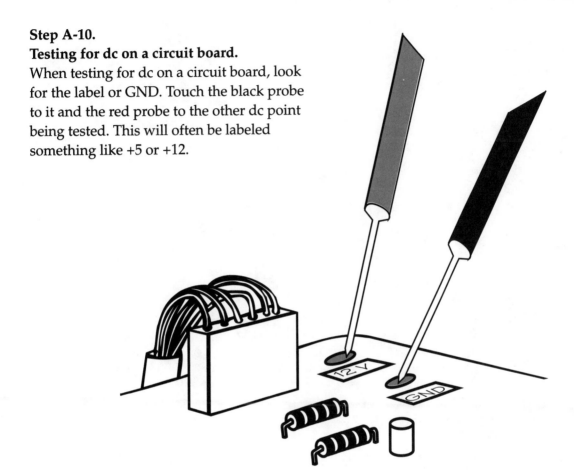

Glossary

ac Alternating current, such as the power from a household electrical outlet. The value is constantly changing in a sine wave.

A/D converter Analog to digital converter. An electronic device used in recording that changes analog into digital (see also *D/A converter* below).

analog A varying signal, in this case such as the signal that goes to the speaker which produces the sound you hear.

audio Of or relating to sound.

battery An electrochemical device that generates electricity through a chemical reaction. A standard "cell" generates approximately 1½ volts dc, and a battery can consist of one or more cells. For example, a 9-volt battery has 6 cells inside it.

bit One of the binary "on" or "off" signals. Generally in a CD, 16 bits make a "word," with a word being a tone. Using the 16-bit coding, 65,536 "words" are possible.

cable A combination of 2 or more conductors in a single casing.

CD Compact disc. Most correctly this refers to the disc itself, but the term has become synonymous with the player as well.

CD-ROM Compact disc, read-only memory. These devices are becoming increasingly popular among computer users. Instead of holding music, the CD holds data (including pictures). With this technology the user has available huge amounts of information in a small space.

dc   Direct current, such as that in a battery.

D/A converter   Digital to analog converter. An electronic device in the player that converts the digital signals into analog signals.

digital   Binary signals in one of two states, on or off, signified as a binary 1 or as a binary 0.

disk tray   The platform that holds the disc for loading, unloading, and playing.

dithering   The almost total absence of noise available in digital recording is disturbing to some. A recording might have additional noise added to it, on purpose, to overcome this. The same technique is used to help smooth the analog signal.

ground   The neutral or return path of an electric circuit, usually zero volts, and usually shown on a circuit board as "GND." In most cases, the metal chassis of the unit serves as a general ground for dc.

land   Flat spots between the pits *(see pits)*. The transition between the two make the actual recording.

laser diode   A laser device in an electronic diode.

ohm   The unit of resistance to the flow of electrical current.

oversampling   A technique of retrieving digital data. When a unit boasts of a 4X oversampling, it does not mean that it samples the recording four times; it means that it is sampling the data at 176.4 kHz, which is four times the normal rate.

phono plug   Also called an RCA-type plug. Characterized by a fairly large center prong and "wings" around the outside.

pit   Impressions in the recorded area, like tiny indents between the lands.

S/N   Signal-to-noise ratio. All analog recordings, amplifiers, etc. have some "noise" (unwanted signal) inherent. The more noise there is compared to the wanted signal, the less quality you'll get.

track   A musical selection of song.

tracking   The following of the recording on the disc.

volt-ohmmeter   (VOM) A meter used to measure voltage, resistance (in ohms), and often current (in amps). Also called a multimeter.

Index